Poor People and Churchgoers

Poor People and Churchgoers

William H. Jennings

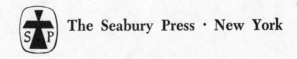 The Seabury Press · New York

An Original Seabury Paperback

Copyright © 1972 by William H. Jennings
Library of Congress Catalog Card Number: 72-81028
ISBN: 0-8164-2075-0
759-972-C-5
Design by Paula Wiener
Printed in the United States of America

Preface

Poverty is our concern in this book, but the book is not about poor people. It is about Christians and how they face the problem of poverty. About a third of mankind is well off, and this is the segment with which Christianity is aligned; the other two-thirds live in poverty, and only a few of these are baptized Christians. What is the relation of the Christian haves to the have-nots? What is our viewpoint, our ethic, our consciousness?

Our concern is not with strategies or programs to alleviate poverty, and if this is what you are looking for you will be disappointed. We are surrounded by experiments or proposals, many of which would be of considerable benefit if priorities in America were to tilt in this direction. The churches, too, have had their fingers in the action and have gained some experience. A perusal of a library catalog shows dozens of "how to" books, including some by churchmen.

Yet, in the area of strategy, the churches are amateurs. Social scientists or social reformers are often better equipped, both in methodology and in experience. Moreover, we are becoming increasingly aware that it is the poor themselves who must have a major part in developing strategies and programs and in carrying these out. When the churches become involved in social action, as they must, they must borrow from the work of those outside who are better equipped to "tell it like it is," to analyze poverty's roots, to express the poor's aspirations, and to point toward constructive programs.

Our concern is with what we should know best—churchgoers and Christian ethics. As we look at ourselves we do not find an encouraging sight. Our houses are in great disarray; we are uncertain who we are and what we should be. We are split between the activists and those who feel the churches should not get involved, and even the activists are often confused over the why and the where. Further, we are coming to an increasing realization that the churches serve their own vested interests rather than mankind, and that religion often fosters indifference and passivity and even prejudice rather than passion for the neighbor. In the words of William Stringfellow, we have come to realize that "my people is the enemy."

Thus it is that in facing poverty, the first item on our agenda is ourselves. We must face squarely the very large problem of our own consciousness and our own stance. We must do some homework.

My special thanks are due to three friends who read the manuscript and offered valuable suggestions—Frank J. McVeigh, a sociologist; Rodney E. Ring, a biblical scholar; and Ludwig F. Schlecht, a philosopher.

W.H.J.

Contents

Poor People and Churchgoers

POVERTY is a personal thing. Poverty is taking your children to the hospital and spending the whole day waiting there with no one even taking your name, and then coming back the next day and the next day until they finally get around to you. Poverty is having a landlady who is a public service nurse, who turns off the heat when she leaves for work in the morning and turns it back on at six when she returns. It is being helpless to do anything about that, because, by the time the officials get around to looking into it, she has turned the heat back on for that day, and then it will be off the next. Poverty is having welfare investigators break in at four in the morning and cut off your welfare payments without an explanation, and, when you go down and ask, they tell you it is because of a pair of men's slippers, that they found in the attic when your brother visited you last Christmas.

Poverty is having a child with glaucoma and watching that eye condition grow worse every day, while the welfare officials send you to the private agencies, and the private agencies send you back to the welfare officials. And, when you ask the welfare officials to refer you to the specialized division of the hospital, and they refuse, and you say it is because of prejudice since you are a Negro, they deny it flatly and shout at you to name one white child that we have referred there. And when you name 25, they sit down and shut up, and they finally refer you, but it is too late then, because your child has permanently lost 80 percent of his vision, and you are told that if only they had caught it a month earlier, when you first made inquiry, they could have preserved his vision.

—Mrs. Janice Bradshow
Pueblo, Colorado

1

On Seeing and Not Seeing the Poor

Most of us are trigger-happy with morality. We have opinions on most issues, such as poverty, and we do not hesitate to say just what is needed. Any man-on-the-street interview quickly brings this out. It is part of our ego to think our values are right and our opinions correct.

Of course, this is also true of Americans who consider themselves Christians. There is often a firm and fixed idea about a "Christian attitude" toward poverty. Conversations with those who inhabit our pews point to this, and it is substantiated by opinion polls and the surveys of sociologists.[1] *

Herein lies a great tragedy both for Christianity and for the nation. These opinions—the opinions of a majority of churchgoing people in America—miss the mark by a mile. On the one hand, they fail to understand the realities of

* Authors Notes appear on pages 113 ff. Notes designated by a figure and an asterisk should be consulted by all readers.

present-day poverty, and on the other, they are based on an outmoded American individualism which is at odds with the best of Christian ethics.

The New Poverty

Michael Harrington, in his *The Other America*,[2] pointed out vividly the "invisibility" of the poor. He argued that the poor today live in center-city ghettos or out-of-the-way rural areas, while most Americans breeze by on freeways or highways and never know that they are there. Further, when we have brushed shoulders with the poor we have not seen them as different from the rest of us, for they do not dress in rags and do not make much fuss. Through the forties, fifties, and into the sixties, poverty was not much of an issue, for the poor were invisible.

Of course, this has changed. Since Harrington's book in 1962 we have had a war on poverty, a poor people's march, a welfare rights movement, and an unending line of witnesses on our TV screens and before our legislative bodies. The poor are far from invisible. We see them. But do we see them?

Most of us still view poverty in outmoded terms.

We are a nation that welcomed millions of the poor of Europe, decent people from Ireland or Germany or Italy or Eastern Europe who settled for a while in the ghettos of our cities, decent people who tolerated bad conditions because they had a dream that some day their children would move up. They were poor and deserving, but demanded no special attention.

We are a nation that remembers the poverty of the frontier—hard winters and near starvation and a lifetime of backbreaking work on hostile land. The settlers, from the colonial period to the twentieth century, were poor and deserving, but they made their own way.[3]

We also remember the Great Depression, the time of 12 million unemployed, of bread lines and Hoovervilles. The unfortunate of the thirties made some noise, but most of them were decent people, and they stuck it out and pulled themselves up by their own bootstraps.[4]

The poor in America's past have found themselves on the bottom rung of the economic ladder. The way out was in climbing. And this climbing had the double effect of strengthening the character of the individual and contributing to the prosperity of the nation. Let today's poor follow the same route! This is the opinion of millions of Americans.

But it no longer fits. The vast majority of today's poor live in a very different world, and the old poverty landscape simply no longer exists. There is a "new poverty" today.[5] *

Let us note five of the most prominent aspects of this new poverty.

1. Vast changes in the style of American life have occurred in the last few decades. From a nation of farmers we have been transformed into city dwellers.[6] * Blue-collar manual labor was transferred from field to factory, with labor unions and worker-protection laws replacing the older laissez faire practices.

Then another great transformation took place, with even greater impact. Blue-collar manual labor, which was the mainstay before the fifties, became increasingly replaced by white-collar jobs. The watershed was the Korean War period, when many GI's returned to find a very different America from the one they had left.[7] *

This white-collar rise in turn produced the educational explosion, as the high school diploma or the college degree replaced experience or the union card as the *sine qua non* for decent employment. Not manual skills but sophistication and "brain work" have become the commodities most required. The future will see an escalation of this as we become more and more a technological society.

This, from the standpoint of employment, is the worst possible time for the poor to break into the job picture. The poor belong to the uneducated, semiskilled, unsophisticated segment of the population. The times have passed them by. What they have to offer, America cares very little for.

2. Another aspect of this new poverty is the plight of the working poor. One of our stereotypes is that poor people today would rather live on welfare than work. The fact is that millions of the poor *do work*. Their work is often on-again, off-again, seasonal or pick-up, and if they are lucky enough to find full-time employment, it is likely to be poorly paid and personally unfulfilling. They are not organized and have no job security. They will be the ones hurt most in any depression in the economy, such as the one in 1969 and 1970. Yet the majority of them want work and millions of them do work.[8] *

For most Americans there has been a steady rise in living standards as we have moved into the affluent society. But the working poor live outside the affluent society and are likely to be doing the same work and enduring the same living conditions as their parents and grandparents. By the standards of the last century, their situation would not be as desperate. But poverty is to a degree relative to the living standards of the nonpoor, and today's working poor, day in and day out, experience this gap.

It was appropriate that Richard M. Nixon, a Republican and a man firmly rooted in the "Protestant ethic" of hard work, should be the first President to focus his poverty concerns primarily on the working poor. Mr. Nixon advocated a Family Assistance Plan that would expand the number of poor Americans assisted by the government to about twenty million, including seven million in working-poor families. Unfortunately, Mr. Nixon's proposal was little more than a beginning, for his recommendations and efforts have fallen far short of what is needed.

3. Old age on a large scale is a new phenomenon. It used to be that a person worked all his life, and death came before the age of 65. One of the happy developments in modern life has been the dramatic increase in the average lifespan to over 70, compared with 54 just fifty years ago. Today there are 20 million Americans in the 65 and over group. And millions of these are poor. One in four falls below the official poverty line, and the number is increasing.

The reasons are not hard to spot. Most older people live on social security, retirement funds, savings, or old-age assistance. All this income is more or less fixed, and inflation eats it away rapidly. Food prices climb incessantly. Medical and dental costs skyrocket and, despite Medicare, can take major sums. Sales and property taxes rise. Housing costs much more.

But what of social security? Is this not intended to help the elderly? Social security has always been related to earnings and often is of little benefit to the poor. If a person had low wages during his working years or for one reason or another was not regularly covered under social security, he will likely get either nothing or the present minimum benefit of $70. In addition, there is a ridiculous "retirement test" attached to social security which reduces benefits if a person is under 72 and earns more than $1680 a year.[9] °

Youth is clearly the ideal in America, and there is a deep discrimination against older people in almost all areas of American life. With the breakdown of larger families we have put them out of our homes, and now we are putting them out of our minds. Meanwhile, their numbers grow and their needs increase.

4. The most spectacular aspect of the new poverty is the new place of the black people. Most poor people in the United States are *not* black (about two-thirds are white). And there are slightly more whites on welfare rolls than blacks. But poverty clearly hurts the black people most, since 31 percent of all blacks are below the official poverty line, compared to 10 percent of whites.

Poverty hits a number of minority groups in America hard—Appalachian whites, Mexican Americans, Indians, Puerto Ricans, older people of all groups. Yet the blacks, because of their epochal struggle to rise out of the older caste system, because of the growth of pride and Black Power, because of their very numbers and the considerable talent which has been manifested in their leaders, because of the very dynamics of the black movement, blacks have become the clearest voices for the poor. They no longer will "stay in their place," for they are convinced that their place does not include poverty.

Because the issue involves blacks so directly, the specter of racial prejudice hovers over all aspects of poverty.

It has long been noted that a great antagonism exists between poor whites and blacks. In the post-Civil War South, where many of our racial patterns were set, the poor whites lived with a constant awareness that they were only one step ahead of the blacks and that jobs and social positions were secure only if the blacks were kept down. Upper- and middle-class Southerners were thus able more easily to exploit both blacks and poor whites by playing them off against each other.[10]

As America has become urbanized and blacks have moved into our cities, this antagonism has continued. In the ghetto areas, racial feelings run high, and blacks and poor whites venture into each other's neighborhoods often at great risk. Many times the inner ghetto is pure black, with some Puerto Ricans or Mexican Americans in a few pockets, and this inner area is surrounded by a collar area of whites who are either poor or nearly poor. It is one of the great tragedies of America's poor that these groups, which should be such natural allies and partners, are unable to work together; in fact the surge of black leadership has often led to even greater hostility and backlash.

Of course, prejudice is clearly not the exclusive possession of poor whites. Prejudice has its origins in the deep and hidden fear and anxieties which lie within us all, and psychological studies have done much to illuminate the roots.

Here, though, we are not so much concerned with the roots of prejudice as with its manifestation. Usually it is directed against those who are different, those who are powerless to respond, those who are "inferior." The poor as a class fit all these categories and are usually a most-satisfying object of prejudice. This pervasive prejudice includes the poor's prejudice against themselves and members of their own class.[11]

Our observation of this fact leads us to an important point which is often debated. Are black people the objects of prejudice primarily because they are poor, or are they poor primarily because they are the objects of prejudice? Some have seen the problem as primarily poverty and have argued that in the American melting pot the blacks will follow in the steps of the other poor newcomers who have entered the American mainstream. However, any such perspective ignores the all-pervasive aspect of *racial* prejudice. Blacks face double odds, race and poverty.

Race is an important aspect of the new poverty. In America's past, blacks were in a separate category, almost an outcast position, and were often not thought of and dealt with as poor people.[12] Now that they have won a victory of sorts in being counted among the poor, their presence overshadows the entire poverty issue.

5. A welfare explosion is upon us. There has been a dramatic increase since the early sixties in the number of people on the relief rolls, and the whole system has become exceedingly costly and in many places almost unworkable.

In 1970 we spent a total of $14.4 billion on public assistance for the poor, and in 1971 this rose to $18.6 billion, compared with $3.8 billion in 1960. The biggest increase has occurred in the category of Aid for Families with Dependent Children (AFDC), under which the number of recipients increased from 3 million in 1960 to 9.6 million in 1970. California and New York, our two largest states, together have well over 3 million people on welfare. Pennsylvania has seen an increase in outlays from $314 million in 1967 to a billion dollars in 1971. Chicago had 485,000 on relief in 1970 and 625,000 by the end of 1971. The figures go on and on, up and up.[13]

What is the source of this explosion? Certainly the poor were poor before, and their need was just as great. But now the attitude of the poor toward welfare is changing, and they are coming forward to claim as a right what many of them were eligible for all along. Crucial in this was the War on Poverty of the mid-sixties; after the outbreak of rioting in the cities, federal programs were set up which hired thousands of social workers, poor people, and lawyers to help families obtain funds. The rolls quickly doubled. By 1970 there was another surge, as the Nixon anti-inflation strategy sharply increased unemployment. With this crush of applicants, many of the legal exclusions and much of the bureaucratic red tape which had kept people off welfare began to give way and the gates began to open.[14] *

The explosion has put muscle behind some long-standing demands for major changes in our treatment of the poor. President Nixon was spurred in 1968 to call for a complete overhaul which would eliminate some aspects of the present system and expand both the numbers covered and the money available. At this writing a reform bill has passed the House but is bogged down in the Senate, and it appears there will be no reform before 1973, if then.[15]

All agree these changes would only be a first step in facing the problem of poverty. This is an issue which will require continuing attention in the 1970's and beyond.

Culture-Christianity and the Poor

So far we have looked at several aspects of the new poverty. Now we must move on to the primary concern of this book, for we are not focusing on poverty per se but on churchgoers and their attitudes toward poverty. How do churchgoers see or not see this new poverty?

Most Americans call themselves Christians. We consider ourselves a "Christian nation," and even if many do not regularly attend church they are part of the Christian climate of America. Thus we consider ourselves informed by Christian values and think of our approach to poverty as growing out of a Christian concern.

This kind of thinking has led Christianity into some of the troubles it faces today. Instead of developing a distinctive Christian perspective toward social problems, drawing upon the Christian tradition and a Christian view of life, Christians have largely mirrored the prevailing values of American society, refusing to recognize that a tension often exists between "American" and "Christian." The result is a kind of spineless culture-Christianity without integrity.[16]

This is seen clearly in attitudes toward poverty and could be documented at a number of points. For our purposes let us note three general American attitudes toward poverty which are generally accepted by churchgoers.

1. The dollar has for some time set the tone of American values. Gross National Product has become the god before whose altar we bow. We judge a community's success by economic progress, and we judge an individual's worth by his status and income. The economic system has become so dominant that individuals serve the nation best who produce and consume and consume and produce. Often education is geared toward producing a commodity: a marketable degree. Foreign policy is often dominated by the economics of our military systems builders or by a concern to protect and enhance the foreign economic interests of American industry. The media serve primarily economic ends, as an evening before a TV set readily shows. Even our religious groups and religious leaders are judged in terms of buildings and memberships and dollars.

The poor, too, are judged almost exclusively in economic terms. They are parasites or they are lazy or they contribute nothing. And in a land where dollars dominate social values, the poor are unfortunate enough to be low in those values which make money—skills, education, organization, social poise, business contacts, power which comes from economic security. Even solutions to poverty are prescribed in exclusively economic terms; it is said that "all the poor need is money," and we are told of the billions that will be needed.

Yet there is much more to the poverty issue than money. Poverty involves a complicated matrix of issues, many of which are only indirectly economic, issues such as patterns of education, the self-image of the poor, consumer protection, political representation, the police and penal systems, the very structure and management of government programs. And among these noneconomic issues which Christians often overlook is the question of the values and attitudes and prejudices of the nonpoor, including Christians themselves.

To view poverty solely in economic terms is a cop-out which oversimplifies. To pass another law or appropriate some extra money is the traditional American way, but it does little for the basic structures and values which lie back of the problem of poverty.

2. We as Americans pride ourselves on being the world's most generous people, ready and willing to help all in need. Our numerous charitable organizations and well-greased fund-raising campaigns are ample evidence of this. In the past, until the rise of the welfare state, our private generosity was the primary source of help for the poor.[17] Still today many feel we should continue to tackle poverty primarily through private charity instead of government action.

Our self-pride in this is truly scandalous. Most of our charity is self-serving. In our churches we do give considerable amounts, but most of this could hardly be classed as a work of love and mercy.[18] ° It goes toward buildings or toward organizational machinery or toward making life more comfortable for those who are already comfortable. Recently this came to the fore in the United Methodist Church with a disclosure that the bulk of Methodist money goes to serve middle-class Methodists.[19] No doubt it will become an issue in other denominations, if we take seriously the servant function of the churches. This is also an issue being raised with respect to United Funds and Community Chests, where priorities often reflect middle-class concerns.

Of course, there will always be a mixture of motives. Just because a charity serves my kids with a Boy Scout troop or helps me with an income-tax break does not mean it is devoid of other-concern. There is seldom pure egoism or pure altruism. But, for a Christian, there should at least be the ideal of selfless giving. This means going beyond the patterns of American charity; it means a far greater concern for those in need.

Christian "charity" is too often a façade of caring which lulls us into thinking we have done our parts and prevents us from seeing the much larger steps which are needed. It may hide a deep lack of commitment to helping the poor. The end result may work against the poor.

3. As Americans our favorite word is often "freedom." We have a vision of horizons in which each individual makes his own destiny. The world is there for us to master, and life is there for us to shape. Our teachers have been John Locke and Jacob Arminius, the English philosopher and Dutch theologian who extolled individualism and had such profound influence on American thought.

We apply this often to poverty. An individual is free to make something of himself, to pull himself up. Even if we can be persuaded that there is a "new poverty," we would still argue that this only makes the task more difficult for the poor. Let the poor try harder and use this freedom to escape poverty!

Most poor people would laugh at this romanticism. Many of the rest of us are beginning to learn differently about freedom, too. We are controlled and conditioned more than we want to admit. From childhood games to voting patterns to religious ceremonies to educational practices to the clothes we wear and the "personnel practices" of our employers, we are to a considerable degree what society makes of us. Our freedom has definite limits. Augustine and Aquinas and Luther and Calvin, all of whom saw definite limits to man's freedom, are more up-to-date than Locke or Arminius.

Herein lies an irony. We tell the poor person to exercise his freedom to escape; yet, of all the not-so-free people in today's world, the poor person is most totally controlled by his circumstances. He is chained by countless intruders into his life—by the grocer to whom he owes money and to whom he pays higher prices, by the ever-present social worker, by the absentee landlord who threatens eviction, by an economy that may eliminate his measly job without notice, by politicians who play with his life like a football, by rats and disease forever present, by the drug pusher or bookmaker who play on his desire to escape. We ascribe freedom to the poor. Many times they ascribe to themselves the very opposite—*fate*.[20] A poor person often feels so completely controlled by circumstances beyond his control that he feels his life to be totally determined and set. A few escape but these are the exceptional ones who are able to foil fate. Most cannot.

These three examples should help to clarify the claim that our "Christian attitude toward poverty" is often in fact a kind of culture-Christianity reflecting the general American outlook. Missing in this is anything of the radical demands of Christian love, missing is any change of values on the part of the committed, missing is any recognition of the urgency surrounding the new poverty discussed earlier in this chapter.

Milton Rokeach, a psychologist who has done considerable research in this field, pinpoints the problem the Christian faces with himself and with his own people:

If Christian values do indeed serve as standards of conduct, they seem to be standards more often employed to guide man's conduct away from rather than toward his fellowman. Moreover, the results seem compatible with the hypothesis that religious values serve more as standards for condemning others or as standards to guide rationalization than as standards to judge oneself by or to guide one's own conduct.[21]

Obviously major changes are needed. Christians must examine themselves and their churches if they are to develop a perspective which champions the poor and challenges the prevailing American attitude, a perspective drawn from Christian roots and not simply mirrored from the surrounding culture.

2

Paths Along
the American Way

One of the best sellers of the early seventies has been
Charles Reich's *The Greening of America*. In this book
Reich discusses three types of "consciousness" in America,
proposing that the "Consciousness III" of our young people
is bringing about a revolution in American society. He de-
scribes consciousness:

Consciousness, as we are using the term, is not a set of opinions,
information, or values, but a total configuration in any given individual, which makes up his whole perception of reality, his whole
world view. It is a common observation that once one has ascer-
tained a man's beliefs on one subject, one is likely to be able to
predict a whole range of views and reactions. Ask a stranger on a
bus or airplane about psychiatry or redwoods or police or taxes or
morals or war, and you can guess with fair accuracy his views on
all the rest of these topics and many others besides, even though
they are seemingly unrelated.

Reich goes on: "Included within the idea of consciousness is a person's background, education, politics, insight, values, emotions and philosophy, but consciousness is more than these or even the sum of these. It is the whole man; his 'head'; his way of life. It is that by which he creates his own life and thus creates the society in which he lives." [1]

There are other terms often used for what Reich is getting at. Sometimes we talk of a "stance" or a "world view" or "basic presuppositions" or "style of life" or "mind-set" or "ethos." Scholars often compare difference stances and speak of "ideal types." For our purposes, we shall use Reich's term "consciousness."

A Christian consciousness in relation to the poor—this is our quest. It concerns more than getting the facts about poverty, for facts in themselves do not determine a person's consciousness. It is much more than deciding on forms of action, for action which does not grow out of reflection and conviction is often misdirected and short-lived. A quest for a Christian consciousness is a quest for a basic outlook and style of life.

This is not an easy task, for there are a number of types of consciousness and often some very questionable perspectives are mixed with Christian attitudes. Before considering Christian consciousness, let us note several other types of consciousness which are common in America and influence the outlook of many churchgoers.

Work-Consciousness

Our Western attitudes toward work began with Luther. The late-medieval society into which he was born had a strong consciousness of God's calling to perform a special task, but it was a society in which the monastic life was the ideal. The Latin *vocatio* was used exclusively for the path followed by a monk. Luther, with his priesthood of all believers, amended this radically, stressing that vocations may be secular as well as religious and that a farmer or soldier or housewife might fulfill a *vocatio* as readily as a monk.[2]

It was under the activist Calvinists that this shift was to have its revolutionizing effects. Especially in England and America, Calvinists pursued their various daily tasks with religious dedication and zeal, feeling that the often dreary and tiring occupations were not so much a burden as great opportunities through which they could serve their God. Thus, what is called the "Protestant Ethic" of hard work and intense dedication was born.

Of course, work is not always the same as vocation, and ideas about it change significantly. Over the decades the emphasis upon hard work has been secularized, and work today is usually performed completely apart from any intention of service to God. For Luther *vocatio* was tied to faith in God, but today vocation is almost synonymous with occupation or job and is spread all across our culture in such terms as "vocational training" or "vocational guidance."

Yet even with this change, still today for millions of Americans work is more than punching a clock or bringing home the bacon. It is a way of life, it is an interpretation of basic existence, it is a form of *consciousness*. Life and death remain awesome, and work is a path of meaning and interpretation. Existence is filled with uncertainty and mystery, and in the characteristically American way, we do not resign ourselves but go out to meet uncertainty by doing—we work. Work becomes a quasi-religion in a secular world. Instead of being a response to God, in the Reformation sense, work becomes an end-in-itself, a locus of meaning and value in a world where traditional religion plays an ever smaller role.

Because work is a basic form of consciousness, it is slow to change and those who hold it cling to it as they would to a religion. This is why a guaranteed income for all Americans is opposed so strongly by so many. This is why the hard hats defend their consciousness against black consciousness and hippie consciousness. This is why there is often a generation gap between work-conscious parents and their children who experiment with different lifestyles.

Yet, from a Christian perspective, this form of consciousness must be challenged. It must be challenged on two grounds.

First, our world has been so transformed that work-consciousness is an outdated perspective which no longer fits. It is a consciousness formed in a day of craftsmen and artisans who mixed themselves and their sweat with the work of their hands to produce something distinctly personal and who could feel a sense of personal identity and fulfillment. Hannah Arendt notes that this was the day of *homo faber* (man the maker), when men worked with tools which were extensions of their hands. Now *homo faber* is largely gone and a more impersonal *animal laborans* is the worker, working with machines and computers and systems which are largely his master and to which he must adjust at every step.[3] Work-consciousness was appropriate for *homo faber* and a man-sized world, but today's world is no longer man-sized.

Most workers today are replaceable cogs in a wheel, and rewards are usually listed in terms of salaries and benefits and time off rather than personal satisfaction. Employers often attempt artificially to infuse satisfaction through "counseling" or "human relations" or even plant or office chaplains. But the fact remains that workers often find the opposite of satisfaction, they find alienation. The Marxists and neo-Marxists such as Herbert Marcuse play on this theme, often with penetrating insight.

Our criticism of work-consciousness is not primarily, however, that it no longer fits into our world. There are many things which do not fit today which we may still judge as valuable. A second and more basic criticism centers upon the view of man at the heart of this perspective. It is clearly a reductionist view—that is, it reduces a rich and varied phenomenon that we call "man" into only one aspect of man's being, and it makes this aspect rule all the rest. We look at each other with this pre-set conception of what man is. We judge a person by "what he does," and our whole social system is based on economic merit; those higher in the social scale are those who contribute most to the economic system. This consciousness becomes the be-all and end-all of the American way.

There is also another reductionism involved. Not only do we reduce man to this one side of his life, we reduce work to only one aspect of its original and true meaning. We reduce it to a market function. Thus in the common view, a student does not work, nor does an artist or a housewife or a

retired person, nor a welfare mother. Yet, these "unemployed" people may have an active and valid *vocation* in the
older sense; they may be involved in personally fulfilling
and socially significant tasks.

It is significant that Luther, with whom our discussion
began, avoided both these reductionisms. A vocation for
him was not the only or even the primary side of a person's
life, and it was clearly subordinate to a higher end—the
praise and glory of God. In addition, vocation was not re-
duced to work with financial remuneration but included
such noneconomic callings as were found in homes and
churches.

Pleasure-Consciousness

While many Americans continue to pay lip service to
work as a pinnacle of self-fulfillment, a profound change has
taken place which promises to undermine this basic element
in the American creed. Man is still economic man, and the
arena of salvation is still the marketplace, but the American
system has become so astoundingly productive and the GNP
has risen at such a rate that an individual's role has shifted.
Today individuals serve even more by consuming than by
working. As *homo faber* was replaced by *animal laborans,*
now *homo consumens* promises to become king.[4] *

We have been taught that the true arena of fulfillment is
in the easy life with all the pleasures and conveniences of an
affluent society. Work is still here, yes, but work is something to be endured in order that we may have the good life
after work. A disdain for work develops, pride in workman-

ship deteriorates, and workers try on every turn to beat the system. And why not, for the truly fulfilling side of life is in the after-work hours of consumption.

Thus, a Sears' catalog becomes a Bible, and the doors of Macy's and Marshall Field's become the gates of paradise, unless one accepts a lesser paradise at a discount store. Television proclaims the path of salvation, and installment buying becomes the means of transport.

In discussing American life, commentators often overlook the overwhelming effect that advertising has had on our consciousness, especially TV advertising.[5] We are bombarded with every trick of the trade to get us to consume the great products of the American way. But ads do not simply peddle products; they instill a consciousness, a life of pleasure where dishes are washed at the push of a button, pain is killed by the popping of a pill, worries are forgotten on a jet-age vacation, and life is fulfilled with a convertible and a can of beer.

A hedonism of consumption embraces our land. Hedonism is a very old form of consciousness which goes back even to the ancient Greeks. It is often skeptical of larger religious and metaphysical values and argues that only one thing is of value and can have meaning, and that is pleasure. And what is pleasure? Some hedonists have stressed intellectual or aesthetic pleasures, but many have focused upon the human senses, arguing that man should develop an optimum enhancement of the senses and the pleasures which flow from sensual existence. This latter type of hedonism is back of America's quest for an easy, pleasant life.

What can we say of pleasure-consciousness? Is this all

bad? Certainly a pleasant life is something man has always dreamed of and is in many ways a boon. Any critique from a Christian standpoint must beware of certain prejudices we may have inherited from the past. Many of our forefathers would have opted for asceticism and a hard and simple life because of a suspicion of things worldly and a love of other-worldly values. This choice is no longer a live option for most Christians, for we have come to view Christianity as being very worldly and even materialistic, affirming the potential in secular life. Further, at times Christians have been overly suspicious of sensual appetites and of even the body itself, because these were viewed as being particularly prone to sin. Again, Christianity is struggling for a perspective today which affirms the sensual side of life.[6]

As in our discussion of work-consciousness, the greatest weakness in pleasure-consciousness is in its reductionism, its elevation of one facet of man's nature to a point of exclusive prominence. Yes, we must affirm an easier life and medical advances and even the liberation of sex. Pleasure is an essential and glorious part of man's nature. But it is not man's primary end.

The consequences of such reductionism are devastating to man's basic humanity and must be taken into consideration in any critique. We note a few here.

1. Drugs occupy an overgrown importance in American life. Young people by the millions are experimenting with Marijuana and other hallucinogens, and the rationale often is that it makes one feel good. The goal is escape, a trip into a realm of ecstasy and total bodily satisfaction. But the larger drug problem is not with our youth, it is with the en-

tire nation. We are a drug society, where millions daily take some drug or other, most of the TV pain-reliever type, but many also under doctors' prescriptions. And why not, if the total aim of life is feeling good, a life without pain or tension, a life of pleasure?

2. Another example is our obsession with sex. The older restraints are passing (and many of them should), and in their place is a view which sees sex as a great avenue of sensual pleasure. The pill and *Playboy* become the backdrop for a mad rush to seek the ultimate in sensual pleasure and to seek it as often as possible. Sex, like drugs, becomes an object of consumption.

3. Americans are becoming increasingly passive and indifferent. We have attained the pleasant life, and we have found pleasure in having things done for us. We are entertained by our TV sportscasts, we are cooled by air conditioners, we are transported by our cars, we feel secure in our insurance policies. We get quite upset when someone interferes with our pleasure, as for example in traffic jams or in power failures. But beyond our own immediate pleasure, we are largely passive. Our moral sensitivity is dulled. This is why the Vietnam war and the civil rights revolution and world poverty have had so little impact on so many millions of Americans. News and discussions of these is there on TV and in our press, but the next moment our eyes grasp an appealing product and we know where our consciousness lies. Paradise, even pseudo-paradise, is hard to leave.

4. Perhaps the most alarming consequence of pleasure-consciousness, and one which ties in with the others, is the deterioration of our public life. We are an enormously rich

and wealthy people, but most of our wealth and talent goes into the private sector. We have plenty to meet individual desires and luxuries but never enough for the great public needs of our day. Our cities decay. Railroads totter on collapse. Schools are crowded and often poorly staffed. Health services desperately need more public money. Parks and recreation areas are too little and too late. Public housing, what pitiful supply there is, is a disgrace. In our typical American style of misplaced blame, we often say the difficulty is with the poor and the welfare freeloaders. Actually, the poor are the ones who suffer the most, for they do not have the resources to withdraw into their private pleasure worlds and shut out the problems of the public arena, as most Americans do.

The Great Quest

Work and pleasure are clearly not the total picture. Millions of Americans are unhappy with the prevailing styles of American life, and there is a great quest for new values and a new consciousness. We are in a transition period when everything is coming unglued and new forms of consciousness are being developed.

It is often said that man is becoming "post-industrial man" or "post-modern man." For over 200 years we have been carried by a view of life which put man in charge of the world and of his own society, a view with great confidence in man's capacities and potential. With this came the democratic state on the one hand and industrialization on the other. Now, however, this old view is passing. Our ways of looking at ourselves and our ways of living are undergoing dramatic change.

There are numerous aspects of this great quest, but here let us note three of the most important.

1. A technological revolution has burst upon us. Vast changes are sweeping over us like a great tidal wave and effecting every nook and cranny of life. Central to this is technology. With it man can go to the moon. With it he can reshape the earth. With it he can control behavior, both individual and social. With it he can even predetermine his own offspring and the future of mankind. Technology is an unprecedented new power which is under man's control, or perhaps man is under its control.

Some view this new stage with great foreboding. Others see a great new world ahead with unlimited horizons. But all who focus on this development are convincing in their argument that it is a new day for mankind.[7]

How does this technological revolution tie in with our problem of poverty? Usually technology is considered in our typically parochial Western fashion as a problem for the affluent nations and for those of us who have arrived at this stage and wonder where we are going from here. Poverty is seldom central, and if it is considered at all, technology is often pictured as a cure-all which will greatly expand food production and industrial output and bring a new day to the poor of the earth.[8] Technological consciousness tends to ignore the fact that technology tends to *increase poverty* and to increase the gulf between the haves and the have-nots and the rich and the poor nations, a point we shall explore in Chapter 5.

2. A counter-culture has arisen as an appealing alternative to the technological society. Found primarily among our young people, though by no means confined to the young, the counter-culture rejects some of the basic premises of our style of life—including work, the American way of pleasure, and technology. It attempts to develop and celebrate man as he is and is capable of being from within his natural self, rather than as he is controlled and restructured by society and technology. The counter-culture is often a world of myth and ritual, subjectivity and psychedelic experience, communal living and voluntary poverty, Zen and Eastern mysticism.[9]

In terms of numbers, there are relatively few who are totally committed to this view, but there are increasing thousands who are fellow-travelers. Many find themselves with a foot in two different worlds—a public and objective and work-a-day world wed to technology and a private and subjective and spare-time world strongly influenced by the counter-culture.

Counter-culture people often express deep concern for the poor and react strongly against American callousness. This concern and sensitivity is indeed welcome and may prove to be a starting point upon which to build. But in itself it is inadequate. Counter-culture people dwell on the "within" of a person and are suspicious of coercion and law. They want a changed society, yes, but by changing the consciousness of people while bypassing the political and economic structures of that society. But poverty is as much a *structural* problem as it is an *attitudinal* problem. It concerns those who live outside the political arenas of the world and whose greatest need is to gain some power, equality, share of the action, and control over their own destinies. The counter-culture is a movement of affluent people who "have arrived" and now want to leave; poverty concerns those who have never arrived and who would like to go somewhere and to have a voice in their destination.

3. The ecology movement is still another factor in the changing American consciousness. The term "ecology" itself was unknown to most people a decade ago. Now every neighborhood and school and town is caught up in a grass-roots concern about our earth. Earth Days have drawn thousands. Recycling is increasing. Antipollution laws are being enacted or enforced for the first time. Unlike technology, which is controlled by experts, ecology is something we all can understand and can do something about. And unlike the counter-culture, ecology is thoroughly acceptable and is given at least lip service by our media, our governments, and our industries.

Richard Neuhaus has written a biting polemic against the ecology movement which contains much truth. He argues that the movement is essentially conservative socially and takes our attention away from the poor; in fact it often looks upon the poor as ignorant and uninformed barbarians and upon the poor's demands as threats to the ecosystem. Survival, not justice, is its primary concern. In addition, its worship of Nature often turns its adherents away from the dirty world of politics and power and class struggle.[10]

Certainly the ecology movement is welcome, and if the ultimate problem of poverty is to be met, any solution will go hand in hand with a solution to the ecological crisis. The problem is the old one of fighting two wars. Interests and campaigns tend to go one way or the other. We find it difficult to look in two directions at one time. Because the ecology crisis is easier to see and touch, we focus on this and ignore the unseen and out-of-mind problems of poverty.

In this chapter we have painted with a large brush, surveying various forms of consciousness in America in search of one which would be acceptable in our search for a Christian approach to poverty. "Inadequate" has been the judgment consistently given.

Indicative of the inadequacy of these American views is the fact that there has been nothing presented in this chapter which the poor themselves would find acceptable. Most poor people reject work-consciousness and pleasure-consciousness as one-sided approaches, middle-class in orientation, and largely inappropriate for their situations in life. But they are also equally alienated from the newer forms of consciousness. Technology, counter-culture, and ecology are also middle-class forms of consciousness, and almost all our endeavors in these areas focus upon the living habits and concerns of those who are comfortable.

The poor are still bypassed and the new poverty is still ignored. Our search goes on.

3

The Marks of a
Christian Consciousness

Christians must find unacceptable these forms of consciousness on the American scene today, while at the same time
recognizing the weaknesses in their own perspectives because of "culture-Christianity." Christians thus find themselves in a position where they must boldly strike out in
search of a more truly Christian consciousness, one drawn
from the wellsprings of their own religion.

The Biblical Roots

A starting point for many will no doubt be the Bible,
since this is the very source and heart of our tradition. Both
Judaism and Christianity arose as religions of poor and outcast people, and both testaments are filled with compassion
and concern for the poor. In fact there is what Harvey Cox
calls a "holiness of the poor" motif throughout the Scrip-

tures and throughout much of Judaeo-Christian history.[1]

The prophet Amos is one among a number of prophets who spoke eloquently for the poor. Traveling from his home in the south, he relentlessly and passionately proclaimed Jahweh's compassion for the poor and judgment upon the rich of the Northern Kingdom.

> Therefore because you trample upon the poor
>   and take from him extractions of wheat,
> You have built homes of hewn stone,
>   but you shall not dwell in them,
> You have planted pleasant vineyards,
>   but you shall not drink your wine,
> For I know how many are your transgressions,
>   and how great are your sins—
> You who afflict the righteous, who take a bribe,
>   and turn aside the needy in the gate.[2]

This special concern for the poor is reflected repeatedly in the great works of the Hebrew Bible. Gerhard von Rad sums up:

The conviction that those whose legal standing was weak and who were less privileged in the struggle of life were the objects of Jahweh's particular interest reaches far back into the history of the people of Jahweh. This conception of the poor practically contains a legal claim upon Jahweh; it was precisely this which made it a self-designation of the pious before Jahweh. In fact, a great number of references understand these poor quite frankly and directly as those who can justifiably expect the divine protection.[3]

As we move to the New Testament, we find a continuation of this theme. Jesus himself was poor, he came from a depressed area (Galilee), and he drew for his disciples those with little or no incomes. His teachings reflect a deep bias for the poor and a suspicion of those with riches and authority. The early Christians, too, had to deal on a day-by-day basis with poverty and tried a number of things. The *agape* feasts of the early church were in part a welfare meal where the poor could come and share without embarrassment. Paul took up collections to be sent to those in need to Jerusalem.[4] And for a while some of those in Jerusalem tried a different tack, the famous experiment in common living:

Now the company of those who believed were of one heart and soul, and no one said that any of the things which he possessed was his own, but they had everything in common. And with great power the apostles gave their testimony to the resurrection of the Lord Jesus, and great grace was upon them all. There was not a needy person among them, for as many as were possessors of lands or houses sold them, and brought the proceeds of what was sold and laid it at the apostles' feet; and distribution was made to each as any had need.[5]

Of all the authors of the New Testament, none shows a stronger concern for the poor than the author of Luke. In biblical scholarship today, the discipline known as "redaction criticism" has done much to help us understand the perspectives and purposes of the different redactors (editors), and this has brought insight into St. Luke. Luke was the first church historian (he wrote Acts, also) and was concerned with developing a theology which would show the plan of God in history. In God's history, the poor have a central place and come under God's special protection.[6]

The word "poor" echoes throughout the Gospel. Luke

pictures Jesus as describing himself as being "anointed to preach good news to the poor." Where Matthew in the Beatitudes records the more pious "blessed are the poor in spirit," Luke presents simply "blessed are the poor." Luke is the only writer to tell us of a "poor man named Lazarus, full of sores, who desired to be fed with what fell from the rich man's table," and of the subsequent events which placed Lazarus in Abraham's bosom. Luke is the only writer to record the parable of the rich fool who lays up for himself treasures on earth. And Luke is the source of the great Magnificat, a kind of emancipation hymn for the oppressed, which includes,

> He has shown strength with his arm,
> he has scattered the proud in the imagination
>   of their hearts,
> he has put down the mighty from their thrones,
>   and exalted those of low degree;
> he has filled the hungry with good things,
>   and the rich he has sent empty away.[7]

These brief references give us a flavor of the New Testament perspective and its Hebrew background. The subsequent history of Christianity has seen a strange and mixed interpretation of their meaning. Often, since the New Testament seems to exalt the poor, poverty has been viewed as a virtue and a path which should be followed by all who would follow the way of Christ. The whole Roman Catholic monastic system has been built upon this, with its counsels of poverty, chastity, and obedience. Protestant sects have also followed this path, advocating ascetic and unencumbered lives, poor in earthly conveniences.

Yet, often the opposite has been the view. Poverty has been viewed as a scandal, and the biblical concern is viewed as a commission to alleviate the poor's misery. Thus throughout much of history, Christian works of mercy and intense social concern have often existed side by side with a view which exalted poverty.

Before leaving the New Testament, one further point must be introduced, a matter of considerable debate. What we have presented is a capsule of the New Testament view of poverty as drawn from a simple reading of the texts. Can more be said? We have summarized a viewpoint, what of the *actions* taken by Jesus and his disciples? Did they put their views into action? Can we read between the lines, can we draw a more detailed view from certain key verses? Some Christian writers have recently moved along these lines and have made Jesus into quite an activist in behalf of the poor.

The argument goes something like this. Early Christians had considerable difficulties with the Roman authorities, and, although they often took their stands, they at the same time were careful not to draw unnecessary anger from Rome. When they wrote, they were careful either to make their writings as apolitical as possible or else to shift any blame to the Jewish authorities. Mark was the first Gospel to be written and was probably written in Rome, following a careful path which influenced much that was written later. But the actual history of the times shows us something very different. Palestine was occupied territory, a Roman colony run by absentee landlords whose representatives the people hated. Roman soldiers were everywhere (they were the ones who kept the New Testament prostitutes in business). Violence and bloodshed and hunger and famine were not uncommon. Jewish guerrillas conducted regular raids against the Romans, especially from the hills of Galilee, the home of Jesus. The Jewish historian Josephus, a witness to much of this, records the struggles in his *Antiquities*, climaxing with the disastrous events of A.D. 70, when Jerusalem was destroyed in retaliation by the Romans.

The explicit pages of Josephus, and the writing between the lines of the Gospels, show that the rural North was the breeding ground of a fanatical patriotic Resistance under Messianic claimants. The massive uprising sparked off by Nero's approaching fall in A.D. 68 implies a long line of predecessors. Several of the Apostles were named by their fathers after Maccabean freedom fighters: two Simons, two Matthiases, two Judases, at least one John. One is explicitly a "Zealot," two are "sons of thunder" who would like to call down fire from the sky. All were looking for an anointed king, legitimated by descent from David; one Simon thought to have found him, and is disaffected when told that this one won't triumph as the world judges. So at a desert caucus the proposal is made to "take him by force and make him king"—the drafting of a reluctant Presidential candidate. A famous saying of the proletarian organizer Tiberius Gracchus is put on his lips: "The beasts that inhabit Italy have their den, but those who fight and die for Italy wander homeless and unsettled with their wives and children." Galilee is the impregnable stronghold of a National Liberation Front, the water that its fish swim in—impregnable because the counter-insurgency forces could never locate any resistance to put down. The Twelve Apostles were born Viet Cong. The liberation movement had a less stable urban base; if we changed the scene a little we could define the rebels put down by Titus the law-and-order Man as Black Power militants.[8] °

Much of this is not new, for we having long known that the common view of a pious, innocent, almost spiritlike Jesus would not hold up. No doubt Jesus did associate openly with revolutionary movements and had considerable sympathy for their cause, as evidenced by a number of references to Zealots. However, as we approach such an argument we must do so with caution, for there has always been a tendency to read our own thinking back into the New Testament. In the first place, we will never know for sure all the details in many of these areas, for the New Testament is so sketchy and does not present a biography of Jesus, no matter how much we might wish it did. And in the second place, we must never lose sight of the eschatology of the New Testament.[9] The evidence is concrete that Jesus was expecting a radical end to life as he knew it and the breaking in of a new day, a new Kingdom of God. Thus questions of guerrilla resistance or social causes in behalf of the poor were temporary questions only. In the ultimate deliverance of the Kingdom of God, the poor would be the chief citizens.

The introduction of eschatology leads us to a final question of the application of biblical ethics to our day. Too often Christians have quoted biblical verses as prescriptions for the present day and have viewed the Bible as a kind of moral blueprint valid for all time. But Christian ethics is not the same as biblical ethics, and Christian consciousness is not necessarily New Testament consciousness. Biblical viewpoints are highly colored by what scholars call their *sitz im leben* (situation in life) and thus are clearly situational. The chief element in this situation was the avidly held view

that the world as they knew it was about to see a radical
change with the coming of God's kingdom. There was not
time for building a more just society nor was there hope in
improving present circumstances; the New Testament concerns focused on alleviating as much immediate suffering of
the poor as possible, but the concerns were short-sighted. As
time went on, the world did not end as Jesus and his follow-
ers thought, and Christians had to deal more and more with
worldly problems—they had to develop more of a social
ethic. Thus Christian ethics and Christian consciousness
have been developmental and experimental. In our day the
biblical record is a valuable heritage, but the Christian community's mission is always to move beyond this and to develop an ethic appropriate for the present situation.

The Responsive Christian

"Responsibility" is a big term in today's Christian ethics.
It is a word with a short history, having arisen in the nineteenth century, when men began to look more and more to
themselves rather than to immutable laws and cosmic forces
as makers of ethics and human society.[10] In everyday usage,
responsibility often implies an obligation to obey certain
rules or to perform in a way which is socially acceptable, as
when it is said a young person is "responsible" rather than a
"radical hippie type." In ethical dialogue, however, it has a
very different ring. *Respondere*, the Latin root of the word,
means "to answer." Responsibility means to give a response
(an answer) to fellow human beings. It involves initiative
and creativity.

Today values can no longer be viewed as eternal truths dictated by God or corresponding to some cosmic standard of truth, nor are they part of man's inner soul or conscience from birth. We are not born with values nor are they instilled directly from some divine source. Does this mean that they are simply subjective, with each person valuing what he "feels" is important, as today's "do your own thing" would imply? No.

The late H. Richard Niebuhr developed a perspective which he called "a relational theory of value." He argued that values are neither purely objective nor purely subjective but are formed and become important as a person enters into relations with other people. Values are *relational*.[11] Niebuhr went on to develop his theme of "the responsible self":

What is implicit in the idea of responsibility is the image of man-the-answerer, man engaged in dialogue, man acting in response to actions upon him. . . . To be engaged in dialogue, to answer questions addressed to us, to defend ourselves against attacks, to reply to injunctions, to meet challenges—this is common experience. And now we try to think of all our actions as having this character of being responses, answers, to actions upon us.[12]

Thus the essence of humanity and of human values lies at the point where humans relate to and with human beings. Relationships are not just forms of cooperation as we seek together some common goal, they are not just matters of convenience or mutual protection. Relationships are our reason for living, they are the ends and goals of our lives. Responsibility (answering) is the core of humanity.

This view of man has strong biblical roots. The Genesis

account of creation emphasizes that man was not created alone but in relationship; "male and female he created them." In the New Testament, man's responsibility to man is found in the neighbor whom we meet on page after page.

Responsibility is also the chief theme of the great Jewish theologian, Martin Buber, in his *I and Thou*. Buber is not concerned with I *and* thou but with I-thou, that is, the basic relationship through which humanity is formed. As he says, "I become through my relations with the *Thou;* as I become *I,* I say *Thou*. All real life is meeting." [13]

This, from a Christian perspective, also ties in with recent interpretations of Jesus Christ. Karl Barth set the stage with his comparison of Jesus with Adam. Adam summarizes all of fallen humanity, with hang-ups and isolation and estrangement and basic inability to relate to other men and to God. Jesus is the new man, the true man, the "Man for other men." [14] According to Barth, relationship is the very nature of God, as seen in the relationship of the Father to his Son. Man is made in the "image of God," and this means that man is made for relationship, both with God and with other men. Christ is the perfect man, and his perfection is in his relationship to his Father and also in his self-sacrificial death for other men.

The insights of these great theologians form a backdrop for what we are proposing. The Christian must think of himself as being always *with* and *for* other human beings. Humanity is co-humanity. There is no isolated I. This is not a choice one makes in certain cases, it is an every-minute thing. It is life. It is *consciousness* for the responsive Christian.

A clear evidence of the presence of such consciousness is seen in the Christian conscience. Consciousness and conscience are not the same, though they are closely related. Consciousness is the totality of a person's lifestyle, including many rational and calculated perspectives. Conscience is a subconscious voice, both reflecting and directing one's consciousness. As we know from Freud and others, conscience is acquired through life-long relations with our parents and peers and others with whom we share experiences, and it is inseparably connected to the very core of a person's personality.

If a person is one whose lifestyle is for and with others, as we have described, his conscience will be responsive (answering). It will not be one concerned with not breaking certain rules or one concerned with avoiding disapproval from others, as is often the case. It will be one oriented to the needs of people. The clear lack of concern for the poor at home and abroad, the lack of sincere moral indignation among many churchgoers is clear evidence that they hear a different tune, that their conscience and consciousness are not those of responsive Christians.

The Responsible Society

So far our discussion has concerned answering as a personal ethic for people who meet and interact on an individual level. We have not yet faced the problem of social ethics, which includes impersonal structures such as government and economic institutions. Our theme has been carried over into social ethics under the World Council of

Churches' "The Responsible Society." This was a theme introduced at its founding in 1948 and carried through in all later meetings. Originally it represented an attempt to wrestle with the problems of the post-World War II world, of the cold war, and of the capitalist/communist debate. At more recent meetings, "The Responsible Society" motif has focused on the problems of the Third World, including poverty, war, economic development, and world cooperation.[15]

In World Council discussions, the term "world community" is often heard. Community goes hand in hand with the responsible consciousness we have been suggesting, and it is clearly one of the big wish-words of our day, even rivaling love. We experience community more as a *lack*, for we feel we are missing it in our disrupted world. Thus it is fitting that a responsible society should be one working for world community.

One of our problems is that our view of community is too small. We think of community as being a first-name thing, where we know people and can interact personally. This is one reason why Buber's I-Thou has struck such a receptive chord. Family or club or Christian congregation or neighborhood or circle of friends become our models for community, and they should. It is in the small interpersonal world that our personalities are developed and our values are formed and we learn to love and respond. This is the *intensive* community.

But the responsive consciousness will never stop with this. Using this as a base, it moves outward to ever larger communities. If intensive community is one's exclusive abode, this gives rise to narrowness, parochialism, even prejudice! The responsive person moves beyond this to include all men, to view mankind as an *extensive* community.

There is a radical universalism in Christianity which means the concern is for all men, including *all the poor people on the face of the earth*. There are many voices today which champion the poor, and there are many motives behind these voices. Most concern for the poor involves some special interest—one may cry out for the Vietnamese peasants because of guilt over the war; one may champion the blacks of South Africa because this makes our racial problems seem more tolerable in comparison; one may help the poor of India because they are so noble and have such a fascinating civilization; one may show concern over American blacks or Indians or Mexicans or Appalachian whites because we have been propagandized and because, too, they have potential for both political power and social disorder. But note, in all these cases, the concern is there because the poor happen to be "interesting poor." [16] The concern is not for the poor person as person nor is the concern for the community of mankind. For a Christian response, world community must be extensive enough to include all.

Intensive and extensive communities are two poles on a continuum and involve very different terms and actions. (See table on next page.)

This outline introduces us to one of the basic tools of ethical analysis: analogy. The intensive, personal, and concrete is the starting point; for the Christian this would include Christian love and the ideal of the Kingdom of God as the holy community. From this starting point, one moves out into larger and non-Christian areas of society and attempts

THE COMMUNITY CONTINUUM

Intensive Community	*Extensive Community*
First-name, face-to-face	Impersonal but functional structures
Voluntary sharing	Social welfare and security
Fairness and honesty	Efficient but responsible means of production
Love	Justice
Brotherhood	Rights
Only a few are close	No one may be excluded
Personal influence	Exercise of power

to exert influence. He finds, however, that his personal ideals are not directly applicable. The world of economics, for example, knows little of love, and the world of government is filled with complicated issues of power where personal persuasion carries almost no weight. The Christian does not give up on his starting point; he attempts to develop viewpoints which *approximate* his personal stance, which are *analogous* to intensive community. Thus, as the Christian responds to the needs of the poor, "rights" or "power" or "justice" are the terms in the extensive community which are parallel to the more personal terms of "love" and "brotherhood." The responsive consciousness is the same; the difference in setting brings about different actions and a different vocabulary.[17]

Some will object that our "extensive community" is inappropriate, for men do not really care about each other apart from their personal relations. It is a dog-eat-dog world in the social arena, each man for himself. There is validity to such a criticism, and clearly a sense of community fades quickly as one moves beyond the small-group level. But it should be remembered that we are operating out of a Christian ethic here, an ethic which stretches itself for the extra mile. We are not describing what is or even what will be. The responsive Christian starts with what *ought* to be. He must avoid irrelevant moralism, of course, but he must not give up on his vision. If his response does not expand into the extensive community, it is too small.

The Listening Ear

An art which the responsive Christian develops is the capacity to listen. One of the great headaches of our world is the excess of words—everyone seems to be talking, preaching, lecturing, writing, shouting. Few listen.

We have long within church circles considered listening to be a means of grace. Priests have spent thousands of hours listening through the screens of confessional booths, and countless lives have benefitted. In recent decades, Protestants have developed quite an art in pastoral counseling, and the first rubric is always "listen." Many clergymen spend a majority of their time in listening to the problems of their people, so confused and distraught in our world gone mad.

This virtue of the Christian intensive community must be developed into a stance as we turn outward to the extensive community. The poor find so few who will listen. They are bombarded with the words of those who would tell them what to do and how to live their lives. But a person who has no chance to express himself, who has no willing ears that will absorb his heartaches and his joys, such a person is robbed of part of his humanity. To listen is a rare virtue in today's world. Our egos cry out to voice themselves; to listen means to be humble and receptive, and this is not a normal human capacity. It is part of Christianity's second mile, a radical stance in a world filled with words. Christians must listen to the poor because the poor need someone to listen.

Christians must also listen because the poor have something to say. We are forever learning the meaning of humanity. We are forever developing our outlook and consciousness. And the poor can contribute significantly. In a sense the mission of the poor in speaking to middle-class Christians is more important than our mission to the poor.

In line with this theme of "listening," we shall devote our next chapter to what the poor are saying.

4

The Voices of the Poor

The late sixties saw two happenings important in any consideration of poverty. One was a direct challenge to our various governments, and the other was a direct challenge to our churches. The first was the birth of the National Welfare Rights Organization (NWRO) and the second the Black Manifesto.

The NWRO is a child of our times. Begun in 1966, it now has over 125,000 noisy, marching, angry members—mostly female and mostly black. Since it is an organization of those who receive public assistance, its aim is to bite the hand that feeds by putting an end to the present welfare system and substituting a guaranteed income of $6,500 for a family of four and an income supplement until a family income reaches $10,000.[1]

The Black Manifesto hit the headlines in May 1969. James Forman, head of the National Black Economic Development Conference (NBEDC), interrupted the regular Sunday worship at Riverside Church in New York City in order to present the black demands. The weeks that followed saw a flurry of activity, with the manifesto being presented to Roman Catholic and Jewish groups, to the National Council of Churches and to several Protestant bodies, including the Lutheran Church in America where it was symbolically nailed to the door. Included in the manifesto was a demand for "reparations" from the churches totaling $500 million.[2]

At the heart of both of these is a claim concerning the "rights" of the poor.

Rights: The Claims of the Poor

In America the idea of rights is best known in the Declaration of Independence, where we read of "certain inalienable rights" such as "life, liberty, and the pursuit of happiness." Being from the eighteenth century, our Declaration clearly reflects the natural-rights viewpoint of that time, a period known as the Enlightenment. Enlightenment men were rebelling against older views which talked about the sinfulness or inadequacy of the individual and which presumed that one's real hope was in following the authorities that were wiser or stronger, authorities like church or king. The natural-rights view argued, to the contrary, that the individual was quite capable and basically good and that all morality, politics, and religion should start with the natural claims of the individual instead of being imposed upon the individual from outside. Thus "natural rights" were thought of as those perfectly obvious and reasonable and inalienable claims which come from the individual.

But these claims did not remain obvious for long. The natural-rights view was idyllic and simple, reflecting the life of early modern man, life before industrialization and technology and supernations and world wars. The natural right of private property may have been obvious for John Locke in the eighteenth century, but in the nineteenth it became confused when capitalists based their accumulation of wealth upon it, and Marxists argued from the same right that workers naturally owned the means of production because it was their labor which had produced the property. The natural right of free speech may have been simple for Thomas Jefferson in the eighteenth century, but in the twentieth it has been so circumscribed by "national security" and "the public good" that we seldom think of it as inalienable.

In effect, we have almost given up on natural rights. We hear many claims of rights, but these are more likely "constitutional rights" or "legal rights" or "civil rights." And this reflects our times. Today's claims are more or less concrete and draw upon the Constitution or upon certain laws; they draw upon the written word and not upon some nebulous and hard-to-define and impossible-to-agree-upon moral claim like natural rights. Ours is an institutional and pragmatic and political and empirical perspective. Our concern is with "is it legal?" or "will it work?" and not with "is it a natural right?" [3]

Almost. But there is a certain ambiguity to the term "rights." There are two meanings—let us call them the legal and the moral—and often the two are intertwined. There seems to be a growing awareness that we have swung in recent years too far to the legal side in our American pragmatism and have ignored the moral. If rights are solely legal or constitutional, it means that an individual has only that which is given to him by the state and is a vassal of the state, a realization which is back of the cries against "welfare colonialism." The individual has some claims apart from the state, and he is often higher than the state.

But this is not the only ambiguity. Not only are there two meanings, the moral and the legal, there also are two claims —a claim *against* the state and a claim *upon* the state. Originally rights meant a protection against the state, for governments were viewed as a necessary evil, and it was a truism that the least government was the best. But within the last century we have begun to think of the state as having a more positive role in human affairs, as an instrument to alleviate some of the heartaches and backaches of man. We have developed a welfare state. Thus a secondary claim has arisen, a feeling that a man has a right to expect something from his government.

These two meanings and these two claims are likely to be scrambled together when one says, "I have a right." To illustrate these various aspects let us look first at our two happenings and then introduce a new item, the Universal Declaration of Human Rights.

1. A welfare mother who is a member of the National Welfare Rights Organization is out to get all that is rightfully hers. She knows that many poor people, because of ignorance or ineptitude, do not get the protection or the

funds which the letter of the law prescribes. So the NWRO has lawyers and counselors who help. This mother is after her rights in the same way that a middle-class professional wants all that the law allows when he files his income-tax return.[4]

But there is more to this mother's claim than lawyers and checks. There is also a moral claim. As she looks at her children, she is concerned with basic rights which are theirs simply because they are human. She does not articulate these as well as the Founding Fathers did, but she feels them nonetheless. It is inhuman to live in a slum. It is debasing to have outside powers control. It is intolerable to be without hope. So she cries out for a decent life and a decent chance for herself and her children, a cry not based upon a written statute but upon what she feels to be human decency.

The Black Manifesto shows a similar focus on rights, but here it is more subtle because we are dealing with voluntary associations and not governments. Many church people were shocked because they were accustomed to free-will gifts to black people arising "lovingly" from institutions of benevolence and integrity. Yet the manifesto will have none of this, for such a view not only continues a paternalistic pattern which leaves receivers at the feet of givers, but it also refuses to recognize that something is *due* and that the receivers have rights. The key words are *demands* and *reparations*. In the words of the manifesto, "Brothers and sisters, we are no longer shuffling our feet and scratching our heads. We are tall, black, and proud." "We have a revolutionary right. . . ."[5] °

Again, we face two meanings of "rights," the legal and

the moral. The moral right to reparations for harm done is as old as Aristotle's "to each his due" and should be obvious to those who accept the premise that the churches have been accomplices to America's racial injustice. But what of the legal right? Certainly the churches are not legally accountable, in a strict sense. The churches in America are very rich and powerful public institutions, worth at least $164 billion and touching the lives of all people at least in an indirect way.[6] Public institutions are accountable both to their internal principles and to the public good. Those outside the churches have a right to demand that the churches live up to what they claim to be in the same way that a welfare mother demands that the government live up to the letter of its laws.

If "legal right" is too strong, perhaps "quasi-legal" is a better description of this claim. The churches have something which corresponds to the state's constitution and legal codes: the churches have confessions and Scriptures and creeds and official statements on issues like poverty. The churches also have something that corresponds to the government's bureaucracies and officials: the churches have officials and boards and structures. The churches are public institutions, something church people often overlook in their pious rhetoric about being nothing except a collection of believing individuals. And a claim upon a public institution is different from a moral right. The manifesto demands not only that Christians support their moral rights to redress of grievances but also that the Christian institutions live up to their words about service, self-sacrifice, and universal brotherhood.[7] *

2. The most significant formal statement of rights in our

century is the Universal Declaration of Human Rights
adopted by the United Nations General Assembly in 1948.
In the distinction between legal rights and moral rights, this
declaration is clearly on the side of moral rights, for what
the UN adopted was "a set of norms with great moral reso-
nance but no legal force." [8] *

The rights in this declaration fall into two classes. First
are political and civil rights, which stand largely to protect
the individual *against* the state or other forces which might
threaten him. These rights—such as free speech, freedom of
religion, freedom of movement, a fair trial—parallel our Bill
of Rights. But the declaration goes further to list economic,
social, and cultural rights, which are less precise and may
not be applicable immediately but should be progressively
implemented. Here the claim is not against the state but
upon the state, for the state must take positive action to pro-
mote them. Let us quote four articles which relate to our
topic.

Article 22. Everyone, as a member of society, has the right to social security and is entitled to realization, through national effort
and international co-operation and in accordance with the organization and resources of each State, of the economic, social and
cultural rights indispensable for his dignity and the free development of his personality.

Article 23. (1) Everyone has the right to work, to free choice of
employment, to just and favourable conditions of work and to protection against unemployment. (2) Everyone, without any discrimination, has the right to equal pay for equal work. (3) Everyone
who works has the right to just and favourable remuneration en-
suring for himself and his family an existence worthy of human
dignity, and supplemented, if necessary, by other means of social

protection. (4) Everyone has the right to form and to join trade unions for the protection of his interests.

Article 24. Everyone has the right to rest and leisure, including reasonable limitation of working hours and periodic holidays with pay.

Article 25. (1) Everyone has the right to a standard of living adequate for the health and well-being of himself and his family, including food, clothing, housing and medical care and necessary social services, and the right to security in the event of unemployment, sickness, disability, widowhood, old age or other lack of livelihood in circumstances beyond his control. (2) Motherhood and childhood are entitled to special care and assistance. All children, whether born in or out of wedlock, shall enjoy the same social protection.[9]

Many endorsements of this declaration have been given, but we need note only one in passing. This is in the great encyclical *Pacem in Terris* of Pope John XXIII which explicitly praises the declaration and begins a discussion of rights with similar words:

11. Beginning our discussion of the rights of man, we see that every man has the right to life, to bodily integrity, and to the means which are necessary and suitable for the proper development of life; these are primarily food, clothing, shelter, rest, medical care, and finally the necessary social services. Therefore a human being also has the right to security in cases of sickness, inability to work, widowhood, old age, unemployment, or in any other case in which he is deprived of the means of subsistence through no fault of his own.[10]

This great declaration, which has received little attention in the United States, has sparked hope and interest throughout the world. Many of the have-not peoples have taken it to heart in their struggle against poverty.

Before leaving this discussion of rights, a cautionary note must be inserted. Any discussion of rights presents considerable difficulty in formulating an ethic for our day. We certainly shall never return to the eighteenth century where these ideas were born. Our twentieth-century view of man has come to accept the role of social conditioning and group dynamics in the development of the personality of the individual; we have abandoned the grand isolated individual, which was the model for the eighteenth century. Thus for us rights are not completely inalienable and clearly less self-evident. Our view is more likely to be relativistic and situational in tone. There may still be rights, but they are not absolute. Thus a discussion of rights may quickly slide into a pitfall of pretty words which do not fit our world.

We have said that there are no absolute rights left. Is this strictly true, could we salvage at least one? Perhaps only one: the right to life itself. The sanctity of life is one absolute we must maintain if we are to remain human. Some of the rights we have discussed are tied to this simple and absolute right to live—decent medical care, a roof over one's head, adequate food. These are minimal rights which society owes to the individual without consideration of the individual's merits or contributions. They in themselves are not absolute but are drawn out of the one absolute right.

Here we have been talking of life in a biological sense. There is also another meaning, a qualitative meaning, as for example when Jesus says, "I came that they may have life and have it more abundantly." [11] Quality of life is not concerned with absolutes with which an individual is born but is something that must be relative to the setting and the society and must be molded in the process. Some of the rights we have discussed are tied to this qualitative meaning—a right to education, to work, to travel, to hope. Discussion of these must focus on society as well as upon the individual.

Any discussion of rights is an abstract attempt to articulate the aspirations and values of human beings. The concern is to enhance humanity. A poor person who talks of rights may not be using the beautiful phrases of the UN or the Pope, but he is often saying the same thing in a more closely personal and human way.

Equality: The Key Issue

At the heart of any consideration of rights is equality. The Declaration of Independence affirms, "We hold these truths to be self evident, that all men are created equal" and the Universal Declaration of Human Rights begins, "All human beings are born free and equal in dignity and rights."

The idea has a very long and rich history. It had a double birth, coming from both early Christianity and from classical Greek thought. We find it in Paul's "There is neither Jew nor Greek, there is neither slave nor free, there is neither male nor female; for you are all one in Christ Jesus." [12] We also find it in the Stoic idea of universal brotherhood and dignity. However, for both the early Christians and for the Stoics, equality was not a workable social norm; in both it was an ideal appropriate only to a world more perfect than our own, for Paul the Kingdom of God and for the

Stoics the Golden Age. In the eighteenth century, with the birth of the natural-rights viewpoint, this ideal norm became secularized and was brought down to earth as a powerful social norm.

In American Protestantism, equality was a key to the Social Gospel program of Christianizing the social order, a view with many adherents at the turn of the century. Later in the thirties it was at the heart of a small but influential movement known as Christian Socialism, a movement which included such notables as Reinhold Niebuhr, John C. Bennett, and Paul Tillich. Niebuhr was the chief spokesman and his eloquent advocacy of equal justice stands as a high point in American social concern.

Turning to today's issues, we may ask what equality means to the poor in the contemporary setting. In getting down to cases we find that concrete application is far from easy. In unraveling the problem, usually three meanings of equality become evident.[13]

1. Equal merit, equal treatment. Aristotle developed the best-known treatment of equality under his "to each his due." Each person may expect to be treated like all others, with only legitimate distinctions being allowed. Under this principle, there is a constant struggle to remove the wrong distinctions and to keep only those which are meaningful. Thus the blacks and the females in our day argue that the wrong distinctions (race or sex) are being used and that they are not getting their due.

The working poor are the best examples of how "equal merit, equal treatment" applies. A man may put in forty hours of hard work, performing to the best of his ability, and still bring home, say, $4,000 a year. A second worker may also work to the best of his ability at a different job and bring home $12,000. Perhaps one is a janitor and the other an assembly-line worker, both socially useful jobs. The poor man, through no fault of his own, is clearly not getting his due. Income-supplement plans are based on this realization. Too high a burden is upon the shoulders of low-income workers. The responsibility to correct this wrong lies with the employer (as in minimum-wage laws) or upon society as a whole, represented by its governments (as in income supplement).

The question of compensatory treatment also falls under "to each his due." Everyone should have a chance for a decent life, and those who start out in a hole should be assisted to make their chances more equal. Thus we assist the handicapped, such as the blind, with special training and tax breaks. We have assisted our military people with the G.I. Bill. The rationale for this has been that a man is taken out of normal life for a few years and when he returns he is at a disadvantage, without the education or the seniority of those who did not serve. So, the G.I. Bill has compensated for the handicaps.

Following this line, many have supported the Freedom Budget proposed by A. Philip Randolph in 1966, a plan calling for $185 billion over a period of ten years to alleviate poverty. Similar to this has been the Domestic Marshall Plan of Whitney Young and the Urban League. And, of course, the Black Manifesto calls upon the churches to compensate for their part in the mistreatment of blacks.

2. Absolute equality. Sometimes equality is used in an ab-

solute sense, with each person treated with strict impartiality. The Supreme Court's "one man, one vote" principle is an example. The work of the courts and of the police should be an example, but unfortunately often we have a double standard because the nonpoor not only are able to afford better legal aid they also consistently receive better police protection.

A few colleges are experimenting with this in their admissions policies. Traditionally admission to college has been by ability to pay or scholastic ability. With a bold new open-admissions policy, the City University of New York has said it would accept anyone, tuition free, the only qualifier being a high school diploma. The intent here is to be equally open to all, including the poor, instead of those classes which traditionally have been tracked to college.[14]

3. Equality of need. A famous Marxist dictum goes, "From each according to his ability, to each according to his need." Because one rejects Marxism does not mean a rejection of all Marxist insights, and here is one we should embrace. Questions of work and merit and contribution and rewards are important and are reflected mostly in "equal merit, equal treatment." However, there are human concerns which lie completely outside the consideration of what is due. Sometimes need itself is the only criterion.

There is a growing awareness of this. Aid to Dependent Children, for all its drawbacks, recognizes that a fatherless child is helpless to fend for himself and so needs society's assistance. And what of medicine? To the shame of America our medical system has been based upon a capitalist premise, and treatment too often has corresponded with ability to pay. Heart attacks and childbirth and mental illness and toothaches are no respecter of persons; they happen to rich and poor alike. A person living in an affluent society may expect decent medical care. It should be a right connected to his person and not to his ability to pay.

These, then, are three directions for the principle of equality. At times this discussion has been a little idealistic and in concrete cases the balancing of claims and actual application of the principle is exceedingly difficult. One finds, too, that equality is not the only consideration, for such issues as good order and productivity must be weighed. The final decision is made situationally. Yet, equality always stands high for everyone who is truly concerned with the poor.

We have seen that this often does not mean a leveling out. But does this mean a leveling up or a leveling down, thus reducing the gap between rich and poor? As we look at the United States we see gross inequalities which cause concern. A clear indicator is the distribution of family incomes, as the following chart shows.[15]

SHARE OF TOTAL PERSONAL INCOME

	1935–36	1947	1968	1969
Lowest Fifth of All Families	4.1%	5.0	5.7	5.6
Second Fifth	9.2	11.0	12.4	12.3
Third Fifth	14.1	17.0	17.7	17.6
Fourth Fifth	20.9	23.1	23.7	23.4
Top Fifth	51.7	43.0	40.6	41.0
Top 5%	26.5	17.2	14.0	14.7

To put these figures in terms of actual income, it is significant that in 1969, 20 percent of all families had incomes of below $5,000, and 19.2 percent had incomes of $15,000 or more. That year the median family income for all Americans was $9,433.

The last time America truly reexamined her social structure was in the thirties, when the Great Depression tumbled many into despair. At that time the gap between the rich and the poor was obvious, and many blamed the rich for the depression and argued for a redistribution of wealth. The solution America worked out was what we call "the mixed economy," a solution we did not march into ideologically so much as back into experimentally without fully examining its social ramifications. In effect, America decided not to redivide the pie but instead to expand the pie. Production and efficiency and GNP have been important; equality has been forgotten.[16]

This has been the traditional line among economists, for it is presupposed that variance in income and status is an essential element to spur economic growth. However, the Swedish economist Gunnar Myrdal takes strong exception. He makes equality the cornerstone of his economic theory and argues that "greater equality in underdeveloped countries is almost a condition for more rapid growth." [17] His primary concern is with poor nations, but he also argues that the inequality of the poor in America is highly unsound economically. Greater equality means better nutrition, education, and social stability, and it leads to a sense of belonging, which is essential for production.

What, too, of the sense of community, which in the last

chapter we argued to be so essential? Great inequalities clearly destroy any sense of community and alienate those at the bottom, a situation much in evidence in America. In Europe the concept of a *floor* has been generally accepted, a minimum income beyond which a family would not drop, a "leveling up." [18] This is similar to the guaranteed income, which is currently being debated in America. Unfortunately Americans usually approach such an issue with exclusively economic arguments. The importance of a national sense of community and interrelatedness should not be overlooked.

The most conspicuous example of our inequality is the great wealth of a few executives, athletes, and families who sit at the top.[19] ° This is unjustified, and a solid social ethic should seek to check this. For example, stronger inheritance laws would discourage excessive accumulation and prevent children from being born millionaires, an idea which is absurd both socially and morally.

This kind of talk makes some people nervous. In American rhetoric the emphasis is usually on liberty, with equality being deemphasized because it smacks of socialism. As we look back at the great debate between capitalists and socialists that consumed so much energy in the West from the thirties to the fifties, we see that capitalists usually championed liberty, and socialists talked more of equality. Hopefully this false dichotomy is passing, and we may talk without prejudice of equality. Even though we may not champion socialism in an ideological sense, there is a positive insight here. Equality can and must be made to work in America if the lethargic giant is to awaken to the great issues of the day.

5

Who Speaks for Everyman?

"Power to the people," "the streets for the people," "parks for the people," "schools for the people"—these and similar slogans are part of the lingo of the poor.

When we hear such protests of the poor, we tend to get upset, for after all they represent only 10 to 20 percent of the population, a distinct minority. We middle Americans tend to think of ourselves as the center of things, for we have made this nation and we represent a sizable majority. If the poor are restless, we will help them to rise to where we are, for we are "the people." We are the norm, the poor are the exceptions.

How narrow this is! If we wish to find a representative human being in America, we will not find him in the suburbs but in the slums. The average American lives in an artificial and protected environment, far removed from the rest of the world. The lives of our poor reflect the lives of most people. What happens to them is what happens to billions. Their voices, their demands, and their anger are the voices and cries of the majority of people on this earth.

The Third World

We have heard these statistics before but we like to forget:

— There are 35 nations (excluding those with less than a million inhabitants) which have a national income per person of less than $150 a year or 40 cents a day. Nearly two billion people live in these nations.

— Birth rates in the poor nations are more than 34 per thousand people while in developed nations they are always less than 30 and range down to 13.

— World population, which was 2.5 billion in 1950, will probably be 6.5 billion by the year 2000.

— In the poor nations, one child in 20 dies before he is one year old, but the figure is one in 200 in the rich nations.

— In the United States we produce close to 11,000 calories in food crops per day per person. We consume 3,000 calories, feeding the rest to animals and exporting some. In India, the total harvest corresponds to 2,000 calories per person per day, nearly all of which must be eaten by humans just to stay alive.

— Also in India, the expenditure on education is $4 a year for each student, corresponding to $500 to $700 in the

United States. We spend more on education than the entire GNP of India, yet have far fewer people.

— In many parts of the world, there are refugees by the millions, with no homes and no income. The war in Southeast Asia has produced a refugee population of 5 million in Vietnam, one million in Cambodia, 750,000 in Laos. Well over 6 million refugees entered India in 1971 from East Pakistan, a prelude to the war which produced Bangladesh.[1]

Such facts go on and on and are indeed impressive. But figures may mislead. Do these not represent the most extreme cases? Admittedly, most people are not as well off as we are, but surely there is a large middle ground of people not so poor. The average human would be in the middle.

No! There is no middle ground. There are rich nations and there are poor nations, and the gap is wide and growing. The rich nations are moving ahead and the poor nations are in many ways falling back. Let us note some of the factors in this widening gap.

1. Technology and affluence mark the lifestyles of most who live in the nations surrounding the North Atlantic, with offshoots into Russia and Japan and Israel and South Africa and Australia. We have come to take our standards of living for granted, unaware that our comfort has to a degree been purchased with the poverty of two-thirds of the human race.

For our modern technological societies to operate as they do, the raw materials and cheap labor of the poorer nations are absolutely essential. The rich nations have billions and billions invested in the poorer nations. The rich nations, especially the United States, control the markets of the world and extract from the poorer nations vast amounts of raw material at minimum expense, while at the same time discouraging development and industrialization and democratization. This set-up is indispensable for our technological societies and the economic return is phenomenal.

A growing number of social scientists are coming to realize that the high standard of living of some of us and the poverty of most of us are related. "They believe that underdevelopment is a function of development and that the affluent nations, particularly the U.S., have reached and can maintain their own level of development only so long as they continue to exploit the resources and manpower of underdeveloped nations." [2]

The theologian Karl Rahner has put this in moral terms:

If we are rich it is because all the rest of us are poor. Because the social, political and economic structures are so unjustly set up that we of the developed nations get richer and richer while those who live in the underdeveloped countries get poorer and poorer.

We personally have not stolen anything. We haven't violated the apparently moral ground rules of society. But those structures and those rules are precisely what is immoral and unjust even though they are largely a natural almost mechanical development in society and in the course of history. If we are frank, we will admit that it is society that steals for us, keeps making us richer—and all the while our consciences are as pure as the snow.[3]

2. The great revolution in science and technology has had *one* pronounced effect on the poorer nations—a marked reduction in death rates. New medicines and medical techniques have been introduced, and the result has been a dra-

matic change in population patterns. Thus science and technology have had an opposite effect for the rich and the poor; they have raised the living standards of the rich nations and have produced a crisis of overpopulation in the poor nations.[4]

Of course, the population explosion is a serious problem in the rich nations, too, but it is catastrophic in the poor nations. A United Nations population study has projected a population of 1.5 billion for the developed nations in the year 2000, up from 1.1 in 1970. This would be an average increase of 1 percent, declining slightly at the end of the century. For the less developed nations, there will be 5 billion people in 2000, exactly *double* the population in 1970. For the poor nations there will be an annual rise of 2.4 percent, declining to 2 percent at the end of the century.[5]

3. The Green Revolution has been hailed as a great turning point for the Third World, and its contribution is undeniably significant. New "miracle" strains of wheat and rice have been developed at experimental farms in Mexico and the Philippines, and these are now being widely used with spectacular increases in production. India, Mexico, the Philippines, Turkey, Kenya, Brazil—these are but a sampling of the nations whose agricultures are being transformed. In the fifties and early sixties, America distributed her agricultural surpluses and prevented famine, particularly in India. But the surpluses ran out, and famine was beginning to creep into the picture and was widely predicted for the seventies. The Green Revolution has changed this.

Yet the Green Revolution has at most bought time. It has forestalled famine, but it has also heightened the problem of poverty. The new seeds require special skills and special care. Irrigation and fertilizer and mechanization are needed if maximum production is to be developed. This adds up to greater and greater dependency on the skills and products of the rich nations.

In addition, centuries-old living patterns are changing. Small farms are being consolidated in order to make operations more efficient. The poor often receive little benefit from increased production because this is siphoned off by those who own or supervise, thus increasing the gap between rich and poor in the poor nations. In fact the Green Revolution has displaced many of the poor from their tracts, and the poor nations are finding increasing millions flooding into the cities, intensifying urban poverty. Francine Frankel notes, many are experiencing "an agonizing change from *security* in the midst of poverty to growing *insecurity* along with poverty." [6]

The Green Revolution holds great promise, but it is far from the panacea many have seen. Land reform and a redistribution of wealth in the poor nations, along with changes in their governments and economies, are essential if benefits from the new seeds are to be maximized.[7]

4. Equality and distribution of wealth are issues even more central to Third World poverty than to the domestic scene which we discussed earlier. In the past the primary emphasis has been upon development and industrialization and annual increases in GNP, a perspective wed to capitalist presuppositions. Now, however, there are voices calling for emphasis on policies to help more directly the poor and marginal members of a society, policies which focus not on

growth per se but upon the classes of people affected, policies concerned with redistribution of wealth and the nature of growth.

The economist Charles Elliott notes:

The fact that in countries that have achieved quite high rates of growth of income per head, income distribution remains highly regressive, and the suspicion that growth leads to increased disparities in income distribution makes it increasingly difficult to believe that, even in the fairly long run, economic growth can bring either stability or increased welfare to those who find themselves at the bottom of the social pyramid. For instance, in Brazil, one of the growth-success countries of Latin America, the poorest 40% of the population receive 12½% of the national income. In Taiwan the same proportion of the population receives slightly over 14% of the national income. In Jamaica, with its tourist boom and bauxite exports, 60% of the population receive 19% of the national income. In Colombia, the richest 20% receive 68% of national income with the top 5% getting over 40%.[8]

5. The international issue most directly related to poverty is the military mania which grips our globe. In 1970 combined military spending stood at over $200 billion. Fifty million people are today engaged in military activities. From 1961 to 1970 a total of $1,870 billion went into military spending, and the UN estimates that the 1970's will see $2,650 billion spent.[9] °

The poor nations are particularly vulnerable. Often their leaders are military men whose paranoia is fed by a military establishment which is mostly used to keep the poor in their places. Latin America is a showcase for this great tragedy; armed forces, since the mid-sixties, have seized power or maintained dictators in Argentina, Bolivia, Brazil, Guatemala, Haiti, Honduras, Panama, Paraguay, Peru, and Santo Domingo.

It is one of the ironies of history that the United States, which has stood in the liberal tradition of democracy and of the rights of man, has been the chief perpetrator of this militarism. In 1970 we officially exported $1.5 billion in arms to the underdeveloped countries; the true total is probably much higher, for often alternate funds are tapped by our government for this purpose, and Congress never knows how the money is spent. By the late sixties well over 50,000 military men from the underdeveloped nations had been trained in the United States, and most of these have gone home to use American weapons against the poor.[10] A powerful weapons lobby exists in Washington which works hand in hand with the Defense Department and the Pentagon to make our capital the weapons center of the world.

In addition it should be noted that since the Second World War, we have developed a cycle in which numerous small wars have been fought in the territory of the Third World with arms furnished by the rich nations. Again we see the rich nation/poor nation gap; the rich watch and even profit while the poor suffer and die.

6. No survey of Third World poverty would be complete without a look at United States economic policies. Basically, we still follow the path set by colonialism. When European nations conquered their colonies, they allied themselves with the privileged few in each colony, who themselves were taking advantage of the masses of poor. The European powers and the native elites conspired to take as much out

of the colony as possible, for their own benefit. Today's patterns follow this same pattern, thus the term "neocolonialism."

The United States is the chief neocolonial power. We emphasize trade and loans and American investments in the poor nations, which means good business for us. In Latin America, directly or indirectly, U.S. corporations now control or decisively influence 70 to 90 percent of the raw materials and more than half of the manufacturing, banking, commerce and foreign trade. The U.S. Fruit Company alone controls over 50 percent of the economic life of *six* Latin American countries.[11] Such statistics go on *ad nauseam*.

Our highly touted foreign aid generosity comes under scrutiny at this point. We began this with a generous postwar Marshall Plan, which channeled $30 billion into European recovery (in dollar values of that day!). Yet, basically this was a sharing among the rich, for the European nations were not permanently poor but were temporarily disrupted. Our aid to the permanently poor nations began in the early fifties, but our generosity never matched that we showered upon Europe. This aid has always been unilateral (concerning only America and the recipient nation), and thus we have been able to influence the policies and practices of the nations to our advantage. Originally our aid was largely in the form of grants, but more and more this has been in terms of loans or obligations to trade for U.S. goods and services and has been tied to military aid—in effect making foreign aid a subsidy for American business or an arm of our military machine. Yet even with this, our aid program has fallen sharply, while need has skyrocketed. For fiscal 1972 our economic aid to the developing world has been budgeted as $1,168,221,000, compared with $1,445,000,000 for military aid.[12] The tragic Vietnam war has taken our interest as well as our money from the poor nations.

Many reforms have been proposed. Senator William Fulbright argues for multilateral aid, as suggested by the United Nations, so that it could be channeled through international agencies without undue American influence. Gunnar Myrdal argues that aid should be in terms of outright grants from governments, avoiding many of the present entanglements. The UN has suggested as a target that 1 percent of the GNP of the rich nations be transferred annually (this includes private investments) to the poor nations. Sweden and Japan may reach this 1 percent by the mid-seventies, and other nations are giving it a try. The U.S. now has a GNP of a trillion dollars, so we have a long way to go. The World Council of Churches recommends that churches in the affluent countries help "to quicken the conscience of their nations to increase their efforts for international aid to a target of at least 2 percent of the gross national product and to improve the existing trade systems and capital investments so they are more conducive to economic growth and justice in the developing nations." [13]

Why is America so blind and insensitive to world poverty? We must agree with Frantz Fanon's claim that Western nations are gripped with a kind of Manichaeanism in which we view ourselves as superior chosen people, elite saviors and rulers of the earth. All others are inferior and do not deserve treatment as equals, for their values and way of life fall short of ours.[14] This is heightened by accidents of skin color, for a pervasive racism still haunts our civilization, and most poor people happen to be nonwhite, both at home and abroad.

America has complicated this with her frantic anticommunism. Throughout the fifties and sixties our primary concern in relations with foreign lands was in combating communism. We have seldom been concerned with poverty or reforms but have supported almost any type of regime which was anticommunist. Our policies have not only increased the gap between rich and poor nations, they have increased inequality within the poor nations.

The Revolutionary Churchmen

In Chile a sizable number of radical Christians have gathered from throughout Latin America, exiles from their own countries. In São Paulo, Dominican monks work with urban guerrillas. In Bolivia fifty Catholic clergymen openly espouse armed rebellion. In Argentina a movement called Priests of the Third World has had repeated confrontations with the military government, and at a mass in Santiago fifty priests were attacked by police and arrested.

In Colombia, Father Camilo Torres, who gave up his priesthood to join guerrillas in the mountains and was killed in 1966, has become a folk hero equal to Che Guevara, and throughout Latin America "Camilistos" is an honorary title for Christians in the struggle for the poor. In Mexico, Monsignor Ivan Illich trains radical priests and laymen at his Intercultural Center for Documentation. From Northeastern Brazil, Archbishop Dom Helder Camara is an outspoken critic of his government and a champion of the poor, and he and his priests are under constant threat of assassination.[15] °

Something has happened to the Roman Catholic Church in Latin America, something groundbreaking and unprecedented. The churches there have always been pillars of the status quo and in many places still are, but a groundswell of revolutionary concern for the poor is rising.

The movement points back to the great social passion of Pope John XXIII, a passion reflected in the "church of the poor" which developed at Vatican II. It continued with Pope Paul's encyclical *Populorum Progressio* of 1967, in which the pope went to some length discussing the plight of the poor and the present injustices and future responsibilities in global development. The movement came of age at a conference held in Medellin, Colombia, in 1968, a conference which issued a ringing manifesto signed by 920 Latin American priests.[16] Today there is general talk of a "post-Medellin Catholicism" in which revolutionary zeal has proven to be a lasting and substantial part.

What of Protestants? Since Roman Catholics claim the nominal allegiance of 93 percent of the people of Latin America, they occupy a position of great potential, and what they attempt will prove to be of great moment for the future of Christianity and world poverty. Protestants have no parallels, for Protestants hold mostly outposts in the poor nations. Yet in their own way many Protestants have moved in a parallel direction.

The World Council of Churches Conference on Church and Society at Geneva in 1966 was a turning point for Protestants. For the first time in Protestant ecumenical endeavors, spokesmen from the Third World played a primary role. The conference was filled with an electric air of change and with a foreboding sense of the inadequacies of past Protestant approaches. Representatives from the rich nations were on the defensive, but they had little desire to defend their nations; those from the poor countries spoke much of radical change, and their views are reflected in many of the reports.

In this new role for churchmen, whether Catholic or Protestant, there is a great sense of past failure and guilt and of the need to create new approaches in the Third World.[17] ° There are strange and powerful messages coming from the Christians of Africa or Asia or Latin America, and often they are being heard and echoed by many of the activist Christians fighting poverty in America. A new ecumenical consciousness seems to be growing with the Third World perspective at its core, a consciousness reflecting the "responsible Christian" and the "responsible society" which we discussed earlier.

America's Poor and the Poor of the World

We began this chapter with the claim that the poor in America are spokesmen for the poor everywhere, and by now the parallel should be vivid. Our poor *are* the Third World, for America's "new poverty" has its parallels everywhere. Let us drive this home by way of a few summaries.

Both at home and abroad the poor are taken advantage of for the sake of the profit of the rest of us. Kenneth Clark, in his study of the ghetto, points out that those who have the real power in the ghetto—the business owners, landlords, police, teachers, welfare workers, pushers, politicians—do not live there. Most of these are outside parasites who come in to feed off the misfortune of the people. Harry Caudill notes the same about Appalachia: "For more than 50 years mountaineers have sat supinely and quietly by and allowed their land, kinfolk, and institutions to be exploited by people who have neither affection nor respect for Appalachia— whose only concern is to plunder it." [18] ° In these comments by Clark and Caudill, the locales are easily shifted; instead of "ghetto" or "Appalachia" read "Recife" or "Khartoum" or "Dacca" or any place in the Third World.

This parallel is also clearly true in regard to welfare. As the poor of America suffer under the inhuman welfare morass, the poor of the world find many similarities in the so-called aid programs. Inadequate, short-sighted, self-serving, and outdated programs are hidden behind glowing expressions of concern and high-sounding slogans, both at home and abroad.

Equality and the rights of the poor are universally crucial issues. Present emphases on production and expansion often bypass the needs of the poor and the demands for basic social changes. More equal distribution of wealth is often a hidden and forgotten agenda.

And finally, there is a parallel in religious leadership. More and more in America those who minister to the poor are expected to be outspoken on poverty issues. This is especially true of black clergymen, where a great transformation has taken place and where strong civil rights leadership is usually required if the clergyman is to be respected by his people. To a remarkable degree the black pastor or the white clergyman working with the poor in America are the counterparts of the radical priests or pastors working with the poor of Latin America or other parts of the Third World.

Americans are unforgivably deaf to the sounds of the world around. While we have been caught in our own brand of navel-gazing, something has happened. Crisis and revolution are in the air. It is a new age of the common man, who for centuries was duped into accepting the status quo. The poor everywhere are coming alive and demanding their rights. It is an age of anger and violence and demands and change.

Christians of America have some listening to do, for the poor on our doorsteps are telling us much about ourselves and our world. We thus return to the angry welfare mother demanding her rights. And the black militant nailing his manifesto to a churchhouse door. This is the voice of everyman in our day.

6

On Starting the Extra Mile

Our concern in this book is with ethics and poverty. Ethics focuses upon that stance or orientation which precedes action. It is concerned with principles and relations and motives. For the Christian, ethics starts with what we claim to be in our churches. Christianity claims there is an "in Christness" and a love and a grace which pulses as the heartbeat of the community. Ethics calls us to this claim and asks whether we are truly Christian ethically.

The Problem of *Agape*

To start with ethics means to start with *agape*—Christian love. Back of our search for a Christian consciousness is the radical challenge of *agape*. This is love which reflects the sacrificial lamb on the cross. It means emptying myself and focusing upon the need of the other. It overcomes selfishness and substitutes compassion. It fights pride and isolation and reaches out to all men as brothers. It goes the extra mile.

Agape is an impossible ideal and it makes impossible demands. It is an ethic permeated with an eschatology which calls for a new day of God, a new Kingdom of God where men will be transformed and where *agape* will be natural and universal. But we live in a world of the "not yet," a world where *agape* remains an impossible ideal.[1]

Because of this, the Christian lives in perpetual tension, a tension between the ideals of his ethic and the mad and disoriented situation of everyday life. How do we deal with this tension? How do we orient our lives in the face of this troublesome dilemma? Generally, the responses fall into one of three categories.

1. Perhaps the most common response in American Christianity is to lower the demands of *agape* so they become more palatable. Love remains the ideal, but it is transformed into a sentimental love which everyone is capable of following. It is commonly thought that the American ideals of individualism and competition and possessiveness are compatible with love so long as a person gives to charities, shows courtesy and helps a friend in need. Christian love is diluted and becomes no more than the service spirit of the Lions or Rotary Club; it becomes a good American ideal which helps self-adjustment and can even be good for business.

2. Not all are satisfied with compromise. Some say *agape* is so radical it involves a totally different way of life which is incompatible with the life of the world. Therefore, withdraw. Form a commune where sharing and brotherhood and

agape can be at least the ideals. Christianity has always had groups with this view, from the Roman Catholic orders to the Reformation sects to the present-day communal societies which dot the American landscape. The secular counterparts in our day are the hundreds of youth communes which have sprung up in our cities and hinterlands.

This approach has considerable appeal, and no doubt many of us have thought longingly of this kind of life. There is a magnetism in the simplicity and sharing and dedication. This way does in fact reflect something which is very much at the heart of Christianity. It might be helpful for *all* Christians to experience this kind of society for a few months or even a few years; we doubtless would never be the same again.

Yet this second approach is no more a permanent solution than the first. The second escapes from the world for the sake of Christian purity; the first accepts the world's ideas in order to avoid the tension. Neither attempts to relate *agape* to the world. In neither is such a mammoth issue as poverty touched. The poor are still there, needing Christians as allies.

3. The Christian stance must involve walking a tightrope. It says a resounding NO to the prevailing conditions and practices of men. But at the same time it cannot escape into an otherworldly position, for Christianity is very much a thisworldly religion. This is the Christian's home and he is responsible, he cares. With the NO must be also a YES.

The great theologians of the past generation, such as Karl Barth and Reinhold Niebuhr, called this a dialectical approach. In effect it says the Christian ethic must be recognized for what it is, a radical ethic which stands at odds with the world, yet an ethic which cares for the world and attempts to have influences whenever possible.

A Note on Theology

So far in this book we have not concerned ourselves with theology, with a few exceptions where an author was noted and God was brought in through the reference. Some may be disturbed by this, for the traditional way of approaching an issue such as poverty has been to set up certain "theological presuppositions" and then to move from these to discuss the "command of God" or the "will of God" for social problems.[2] ° Traditionally, in Protestant circles at least, ethics has been a subtopic under theology; understanding God comes first, and then an ethic grows out of this understanding.

Our procedure has been deliberate. In our day the question of God is one of the thorniest of all, and traditional language often causes more confusion than clarity. Certainly the "will of God" and the "command of God" are symbolic expressions which come from thinking of God as a Person. But is God a Person and does God will? Perhaps such terms are basically human projections, and we are simply describing God as an idealized human being, as Feuerbach and Freud would maintain. Perhaps different terms are needed in our day.

This is not to say that theology is irrelevant for ethics and that we are left with a simple ethical humanism. The churches are not Ethical Culture societies. There are still basic theological dimensions to Christian ethics, but we must be honest and careful in how we state them.

Mystery and holiness are still large elements in human consciousness, as young people today are quick to point out. Perhaps such terms as "Ground of Being" or "Eternal Thou" or "Wholly Other" or "World Soul" sound different from our biblical "God" or "Father," but the intent is the same—to relate to and respond to the mysterious and holy source of life, which is so far beyond our understanding as to be impossible to capture in words. This mysterious Other is not a being apart from the world but is inseparable from life. We and the Other are intertwined in existence. This is the meaning of the Christian myth of God's coming down to be incarnate in flesh. God is with us, the mysterious and holy presence at the heart of life.

This mysterious Other repeatedly draws our response. No one is neutral, we must respond in some way—by traditional faith-statements, by inner struggles and doubts, by agnostic or defiantly atheistic stances. The Judaeo-Christian tradition has fostered a positive response, suggesting that the believer is responding to One, who responds to man. And, again using our method of analogy, our response to our fellow man is an echo of our response to the mysterious Other. Both Martin Buber and H. Richard Niebuhr were quick to point out that a true I-Thou relationship is impossible as long as there are only two isolated individuals. There must also be an "Eternal Thou" to whom we respond and who responds to us.

How does one meet this mysterious Other? There are usually three avenues. Many proceed through nature. The great

Jahweh of the Hebrew Bible may have originally been associated with a mountain, with its awesome heights and rumbling thunder. The Psalmists repeatedly list the hills and other works of Jahweh's hands as appropriate meeting places. In our day, this is a favorite path of nature lovers and has become very big in the ecology movement.

A second avenue is within the self. One focuses upon the inner self and contemplates the mysteries of the psyche, postulating that what is within corresponds to the great mind and plan of the universe. This is a favorite path of many mystics, both Eastern and Western.

A third path is parallel to what we have been proposing in this book. One meets the mysterious Other not primarily in nature or in the self but in the brother. Life is basically meeting and interaction, and the dignity and holiness of other human beings is the point at which one knows the mystery of life. It is noteworthy that the great Hebrew theologians, while at times flirting with both nature and the self as avenues for meeting Jahweh, consistently emphasized community and the fellow man as the most appropriate. This is also the insight of Jesus, "Truly, I say to you, as you did it to one of the least of these my brothers, you did it to me." [3] And, of course, it is the wisdom of Christian theology which argues that a response to a man, Jesus Christ, is a response to the source of our very being.

Much could be said about this, but we need note only three brief points here.

1. Here we see the religious significance of community. Community is not just a bit of social engineering. It becomes a locus for the mystery of life, for it is here that we

undertake our common searches and share our obligations and destinies. It is in intensive community that *agape* and a Christian consciousness are formed, and it is from intensive community that the Christian moves out in search of the wider, extensive communities we noted earlier.

In Christian community the sacrament of the Lord's Supper has always been a high point, both symbolizing and also within itself helping to bring about community. This sacrament has dynamic implications and is a powerful base for social concerns. The sacrament proclaims: " 'Those who are starving out there are also members of your fellowship. They are no further away from you than those who live in your parish.' Thus every Communion has to do with development aid, and our whole church financial policy is confronted by the challenge directed to us . . . to make a 'visible sacrifice.' " [4]

2. We are again brought face to face with the question of eschatology. The eschatology of the New Testament is clearly social, emphasizing a holy community and picturing this in terms of heavenly banquets and eternal group-singing. For the Christian this social emphasis will always be central, but today a Christian is likely to have difficulty with New Testament eschatology because it does predict a radical end to life as we know it and a glorious new day of God.

Today we must reinterpret this eschatology to some degree, recognizing that the early Christian view of the world was somewhat different from ours and that much of the New Testament cannot be taken literally. The problem with the older view is that it neglected this world to some extent in its longing for the otherworldly new kingdom. In any reinterpretation, this world and human relations as they exist in this life must be the focus. Yet a reinterpretation does not negate the importance of eschatology, for the New Testament talk about a "new day" involves some very powerful symbolism which directly ties to our problem of poverty. The "coming of God" and "God's reign" can be translated something like this: "Our search for the holiness of life involves a hope that a new humanity is possible and a desire for a new day when poverty and war and enmity will diminish."

The eschatological element remains, reminding us that the Christian vision and man's reality are two very different things. For us eschatology forever reminds us that the conditions of mankind are not what they ought to be, forever warning us of culture-Christianity, forever motivating us to respond to our fellow men. As Helmut Gollwitzer notes, "Eschatology and social ethics belong together—this is one of the most important realizations of contemporary theology." [5]

The clearest example of this is what is now happening in the Roman Catholic Church. Before the great Second Vatican Council (1962–65), the Catholic Church was entangled in an otherworldly perspective and was clearly out of touch with today's world. But Vatican II was a happening which brought the church squarely into today's problems. While retaining its "not of this world" perspective to a degree, the Council said, "The expectation of a new earth must not weaken but rather stimulate our concern for cultivating this one. For here grows the body of a new human family, a body which even now is able to give some kind of foreshadowing of the new age." [6] In other words, God and the true community of God are found here and now among the poor of the earth and those who seek to serve the poor. The biblical "holiness of the poor" rushes in with a twentieth-century garb.

George Lindbeck, a Protestant scholar, interprets this "secular mission" based upon "thoroughly eschatological teaching" as the great central emphasis of the Council, an emphasis which has changed the very nature of the Roman Catholic Church: "In short, to repeat the phrase which seemed to move the assembled bishops in the Council more than any other, the church is in its essence and must become manifestly, 'the church of the poor' and the oppressed, not of the rich and the oppressors. Many bishops insisted this should be true not only within each country but also on an international scale. The church should identify itself more with the poor, underdeveloped countries than with the rich, Western, purportedly Christian ones." [7]

3. Along these lines we also see the importance of grace. Eschatology implies that there is something more than the simple responsibility of man, that there is a hope and a potential which exceeds man's grasp. It is the extra mile of Christian *agape,* for mere humans can hardly be expected to sacrifice themselves to others, and yet we know that this sacrifice of self is of the essence of living.

One of the strongest points made by the idea of grace is a negative one. We urgently need it. Our lives are obviously so weak and inferior and fall short of what we know they should be, so filled with what religion calls sin. If we look with a hard-nosed approach at ourselves and our world, there is no room for optimism.[8] We can only agree with the existentialists, who talk so much of absurdity. Obviously there is no solution to world poverty, and the situation grows more grave each day. The racial crisis deepens. Yet we hope. Hope is a gift of grace, a spark of life, and a surprise that impels us on. In spite of the odds, men seem to be born ever anew within their communities where they lean upon each other and hope continues.

Being a gift, grace knows little of human merit. This fact should have a profound impact upon the Christian's response to poverty. Christians talk much of the grace of God (Protestants even talk of grace *alone*), yet they turn around and judge their fellow men almost exclusively in terms of merit. Grace shifts the emphasis from worth and merit to need and dignity.

This brief discussion has hardly brought us closer to the question of God. But it has pointed to a way that more and more Christians are following as they struggle. In a sense, ethics does not grow out of faith in God any more than faith in God grows out of ethics. The two are intertwined. To talk of God is to talk of man's relation to man; God-talk is also talk about man. Yet, on the other side of the coin, ethics involves an *ought* which draws us to think of the source of life and obligation, the mysterious ultimate relation which we all share.

The Churches and Ethical Dialogue

The path we have outlined is filled with difficulties. It has no easy answers, no blueprint of a perfect society. It is a path to be cleared as one goes along, not a highway with large signs. It involves searching and questioning concerning the meaning of Christian faith in today's world. It involves ongoing ethical dialogue.

Among Christian ethicists, James M. Gustafson has written most cogently on this point, arguing that the internal life of a church should be "analogous to the life of a serious moral agent."[9]° Just as a sensitive individual considers different options, continuously examines his own values, discusses with others, weighs his own conscience—so a church should be a community involved in a similar ongoing process. Gustafson argues that such a community is more likely to have a clear sense of its own reason-for-being, its intentions and goals. And when this is true it is less likely simply to reflect the values of the larger society. It establishes some independence and integrity.

This ethical dialogue has two thrusts. First it is dialogue among Christians within the churches. The churches are not depositories of answers to man's problems but are communities of people on their way, people seeking and sharing. Christians must openly and sincerely discuss questions like the meaning of God, the scope of responsibility, the forms of *agape*. Christians must seek their own identity through dialogue.

Dialogue has another aspect, equally important. It is also dialogue of the churches with the world. Here the voices of the poor have much to contribute, as well as many other developments of the modern era. The Dutch theologian Edward Schillebeeckx states this well: "The relationship of the Church and the world is thus no longer the relationship of a 'teaching' Church to a 'learning' world, but the interrelationship of dialogue in which both make a mutual contribution and listen sincerely to each other." [10] Church people have much to learn. The change in eschatology which we have described makes us take "the world" much more seriously than ever before, for this is the arena of the new humanity.

Yet in spite of this obvious double need for ethical dialogue, it hardly exists in most of our churches. The desire for dialogue is absent, and the structures of the churches discourage it. Basic changes are needed. Let us make a few observations about the setting for dialogue in the churches.

1. The sermon must be amended or abandoned if genuine dialogue is to take place. In Protestantism the emphasis upon the Bible and the preached Word of God and in Catholicism the authoritarianism of the hierarchy have encouraged a passive and receptive attitude among lay people. The pulpit has been placed above the people and religious truths have been handed down with a "thus says the Lord." After a lifetime of this, it is no wonder churchgoers are so hard to draw out of their shells and into dialogue. In some places changes have been attempted through dialogue sermons or sermon feedback, but even these have had limited success. Perhaps the sermon itself should be shelved as a remnant from a former authoritarian world. Pastors should struggle against their own authority hang-ups and develop as a primary ministerial function their capacities to elicit critical and responsible thought and discussion among their people.

2. The old sacred/secular, church/state, and two-kingdoms dualisms must be reexamined. American Christianity has been strongly influenced by the Methodist and Baptist

outlook of the nineteenth century which proclaimed "the sole business of religion is to save souls," and it has often been seeped in a warm pietism which looks for inner faith but maintains a hands-off policy toward worldly affairs. Because of this split view, there has been a tendency to consider things pertaining to the secular or to the state as being off-limits. Thus many issues, such as those connected with poverty, are not brought into the churches.

3. Church finances should be amended so that ethical dialogue and individual decision are encouraged. There is usually a unified budget, with offering envelopes mislabeled "current" and "benevolence." Many churchgoers have only a vague idea of where their money goes, and giving becomes a sop for the conscience rather than a calculated decision. There should be a variety of causes, with various opportunities. Paul C. Empie, for example, notes that during and after World War II Lutheran World Action was a special appeal in the Lutheran churches, and much was done to inform people of its program. "They learned what Lutheran World Action was about—and not only got excited about it; they responded far more liberally in proportion to their means than is the case today." Later this became a regular budget item and disappeared from discussion and concern, except in the upper echelons.[11] Individuals should have a clear chance to choose how much to give to world relief or to lobbying in Washington or to inner-city work or to colleges and homes for the aged or to building upkeep. This might cause chaos in the current church bureaucracies but some chaos can at times be creative.

4. Attempts should be made to hear opinions other than our own. Controversial speakers and programs should be ar-

ranged. The old "don't rock the boat because it will cost money and members" attitude must go. A starting point might be spokesmen for the Black Manifesto or a welfare rights organization. Black "Uncle Toms" or speakers who can be predicted and controlled will not do. To a considerable degree churches still maintain the old practice in which blacks were invited to visit or sing but never allowed to speak, only now it is "radicals" or "dissenters" rather than blacks. Ethical dialogue is enhanced when we are no longer shocked or enraged at a new view; we should have heard it all and on a regular basis if we are to think and act responsibly.

Some will reply that such proposals as these four are either too little or too late, for the churches are too far gone for dialogue and social impact. Our earlier discussion of culture-Christianity would support such doubt. Some have voted with their feet and left the churches to seek a secularized form of Christianity or else a more flexible and lively form of community in experimental underground church groups.[12]

Certainly this task faces enormous odds, and if churches do become centers of ethical dialogue, they themselves will have to change significantly in the process. But there are many who feel that religious community is essential for Christianity just as it is for Judaism. In addition, Christian communities can and should have a significant impact upon society, an impact which is not possible for isolated individuals. Among the institutions of the American nation, there are few which have a built-in potential for discussion of the primary issues of the day. Just as what America is and does will influence the rest of the world, what America's churches are and say will influence America.

On Doing

Dialogue is no end in itself, for it must be directed toward specific and concrete action. Dialogue which is not tied to action is irresponsive. Dialogue which does not have social consequences is no more than private recreation and does not reflect the true nature of our religion. Action is an essential arm of dialogue, for it feeds back and helps us to test our thoughts and our sincerity and our wisdom.

A good case can be made that when there is solid ethical dialogue, constructive action will more likely follow. One reason why churchgoers are so passive and inactive on social issues is that they are uncertain about the "why," unsure of how their faith should plug in. Churchgoers are often passive because the groundwork has not been laid through dialogue.[13] * It is a well-established dictum of social science that people are more likely to care, to mature, to respond, to act, if they are part of the dialogue all along the way. In Gustafson's words, "When we begin to take initiative in reflection, we are likely to take initiative in action. We can become an initiating community rather than a reactive community. Perhaps the church will not be as boring to thinking and acting laymen as it often is now; perhaps it will look less like an archaic museum piece and more like a confident community that knows why it exists." [14]

To a degree Christian action against poverty is not new. We have had a long and at times estimable history, from hospitals to children's homes and old people's homes to handouts for the needy. We should not criticize this but note that in our day such a works-of-mercy understanding of action accepts without question the social system; in fact it may even serve the present social system by assuaging its ills.

The "Thanksgiving basket detail" is often used as an illustration of the inadequacy of the old way, and my experience one year with this left an indelible impression. We took a turkey and all the trimmings to a family with ten children. They lived in a hovel, but it was the best they could do; the husband worked long hours as a janitor, but his pay could hardly feed his family, much less buy clothes or house them. Such service often makes the Christian feel good. But our finest service to this family would have been to try to do something about an economic system which leaves many in such a plight and to do something about a governmental system which, as many spokesmen for the poor note, means "welfare for the rich and free enterprise for the poor."

Older ways of facing poverty, although they may continue, address only the older poverty and are inadequate to today's needs; they must be augmented with brave and venturesome new approaches which more directly attack the new poverty. There are several points to be noted here about Christian action.

1. Christian social action today must be concerned with social structures. Usually it is the very organization of the society which determines poverty. Christian concern must be directed toward this very complicated larger issue of how our society operates.

The more-far-reaching proposals would include such

things as a new constitution or more public ownership or control of major industries. Tamer suggestions might include a guaranteed income, more political clout for the cities, reform in the House of Representatives, a shake-up of local city halls when they are controlled by propertied classes, more legal recognition of the rights and voices of the poor. This is the work of politics, work which disturbs and brings slow results and little praise. But in our day it is often the greatest form of service. "As a Church we must be clear that we have to move *from service understood as serving the present order to service in the name of structural change.*" [15] This should be a clear and urgent conclusion from our study.

2. If structural change is to occur, groups such as the churches must always be one step ahead of politics as we find it. We must be the avant-garde, always critical of government for being too slow and too irresponsive:

Certain things are inherently difficult for government. Being by design a protective institution, it is not good at innovation. It cannot really abandon anything. The moment government undertakes anything, it becomes entrenched and permanent. Better administration will not alter this. Its inability to innovate is grounded on government's legitimate and necessary function as society's protective and conserving organization. [16]

Because this is the nature of government, especially in our day, politics in the broader sense will always involve groundbreaking groups willing and able to move ahead, to experiment, to put their efforts and money into new avenues which, hopefully, some day governments will follow.

To a dramatic new degree, some church groups in fact

today are attempting to play this role. When the War on Poverty was initiated in 1964, churches jumped on the bandwagon and became involved in Head Start or the Job Corps or day-care centers or migrant work. In this they were cooperating with government and following the traditional path of service. But then the War on Poverty became bogged down, and it was evident that government was going to do little. At that point a change occurred in the perspective of some churches. They began to support Black Power or the NWRO or other such groups. In some of the national church bodies a movement was begun to use the billions of church dollars invested in banks and corporations to pressure changes in business policies. There was a call for more effective lobbying by church groups in Washington and at state capitals. More and more the emphasis has been placed on direct social change and less and less on social service.[17]

This new role is hotly debated and has split many congregations and church bodies and is the hottest social issue in the churches since the Social Gospel period. To date it is championed by only a few congregations and a minority of church officials, but it has great potential. In some places it is belatedly forcing the churches into ethical dialogue.

3. Action on behalf of the poor means that we do not do so much *for* the poor as *with* the poor. There is a growing consensus among activists that we have often been misdirected in our concern to do things for the poor. We have often practiced a paternalism which has done more harm than good. The poor have their aspirations, their values, their needs, their voice. Action should be concerned with aligning ourselves alongside the poor to enable them to gain

the power and influence they need. To do *for* means to treat the poor person as object, as thing. To do *with* is to treat him as subject and to raise the possibility of interrelationships and response—the responsive Christian approach.

In the much-maligned War on Poverty there was one program which was imaginative and notedly controversial. It was the Community Action Program and was defined as follows: "The term 'Community Action Program' means a program which is developed, conducted, and administered with maximum feasible participation of residents of the areas and members of the groups served." [18] "Maximum feasible participation" became a hot potato and was strongly opposed by local mayors and others who saw a threat to their power. In practice it meant getting the poor on local poverty boards and helping the poor to organize so they would have a voice and power in determining their own destiny.

The churches developed this principle in some places before it was taken up by the War on Poverty, and it is still seen in much church work among the poor—for example, with grape workers in California, with the Mississippi Delta ministry in the South, with support for Saul Alinsky in Chicago and Rochester, with work among migrants, and with inner-city work in a number of places.[19]

We have in this study mentioned a number of additional areas which could involve maximum feasible participation and a standing *with* the poor—from guaranteed income to welfare rights organizations, from reform of foreign aid to college admissions, from income supplements to the Black Manifesto, from medical care at home to a greater voice for the poor in international affairs. In all of these the churches should stand in the avant-garde, leading and pressuring for responsible politics and fighting for major structural changes in our society.

Throughout this book we have focused our attention on ethics and poverty. We have attempted to develop a challenge both to average churchgoers and to their leaders. Churchgoers must awaken to the great discrepancy between their attitudes and the radical call of the Christian religion. But this has not been meant as just another browbeating of churchgoers; it is also a call to leaders to realize the inadequacies of past activist approaches. Too often leaders have developed programs and proclaimed these to their people without opening up the ethical issues.

To develop within the churches communities of ethical dialogue is essential in any reform of the American churches. And since ethics is at its heart concrete and situational, poverty is a vital occasion for such dialogue.

Can the churches develop this capacity and play an important role in facing poverty? Perhaps this is the most disabling problem of all, for the churches are fragmented and faced with self-doubt. In this period of great religious change they are losing confidence. Yet resignation is not a live option. If we still hold to Christianity and are committed to its transforming power in the world, we must move ahead with the task: "For there is nothing that so paralyzes and corrodes the Christian Church in its old age as the spirit of resignation. It hardly believes that it still has any kindling power. But we cannot at the same time be a Christian and give up hope." [20]

Appendix: Some Statistics

The Poor in the United States

The federal government's classification is the one most often used for poverty, and it uses a sliding scale based on the number of members in a family and the rise in living expense. In January 1971, a nonfarm family of 4 with an income of less than $3,800 was considered poor, as was a farm family with less than $3,200. Even with this low cut-off, there were 25.5 million poor people in the United States in 1970. There were 17.5 million whites in this total (67%) and 7.7 million blacks.[1]

Domestic Welfare Programs

There are numerous government projects which directly or indirectly help the poor. Unemployment insurance, for example, helped 1,804,631 workers in 1970 with average weekly benefits of $50.31; it should be noted, however, that not all the unemployed are poor and that there is a limit to the number of weeks a person may draw this.[2] Further, medicare is partly financed by public funds, and in addition, there are provisions for hospitals, public health, food stamps, and special programs for the poor in some schools.

The most direct aid for the poor is under the categories of Public Assistance and Welfare. There are five types of assistance here. The first four are joint federal and state undertakings (on the average the state provides 45% of the funds, the federal government 55%). General Assistance is from some combination of state, county, and local funds.

PUBLIC ASSISTANCE AND WELFARE PROGRAMS [3]
1970

	Persons (average)	Total Paid Out	Average Monthly Benefit
1. Old Age Assistance	2,081,000	$1,861,074,000	77.60
2. Aid to the Blind	81,000	98,280,000	104.35
3. Aid to the Permanently and Totally Disabled	933,000	984,995,000	96.55
4. Aid to Families with Dependent Children	9,657,000 (2,552,000 families)	4,852,184,000	49.50 (187.30 per family)
5. General Assistance	1,062,000	618,677,000	57.75

World Poverty

One of the ways of measuring world poverty is by per capita gross national product. This, of course, does not indicate distribution within a country, where great inequalities are usually the case, but it does show the meager resources in many nations. The statistics are from 1969, with growth rates measured from 1960 to 1969.[4] Excluded are nations with less than a million people and those with per capita GNP's of 300 or over.

VERY POOR COUNTRIES

	Popu-lation (add 000)	GNP Per Capita (U S $)	GROWTH RATES Pop'n (%)	GROWTH RATES GNP Per Capita (%)
Afghanistan	13,975	under 100	2.0	0.3
Algeria	13,349	260	2.4	
Angola	5,430	210	1.3	1.4
Bolivia	4,804	160	2.6	2.4
Brazil	92,282	270	3.2	1.4
Burma	26,980	under 100	2.1	1.8
Burundi	3,475	under 100	2.0	0.0
Cameroon	5,736	150	2.1	2.0
Central African Rep.	1,518	130	2.4	0.0
Ceylon	12,244	190	2.4	2.1
Chad	3,510	under 100	1.5	−1.3
China (Mainland)	740,000	under 100	1.5	0.8
Colombia	20,463	290	3.2	1.5
Congo, Dem. Rep. of	17,900	under 100	2.1	0.2
Cuba	8,513	280	2.5	−3.2

VERY POOR COUNTRIES (*Continued*)

	Population (add 000)	GNP Per Capita (U S $)	GROWTH RATES	
			Pop'n (%)	GNP Per Capita (%)
Dahomey	2,640	under 100	2.9	0.9
Dominican Republic	3,951	280	3.0	0.4
Ecuador	5,890	240	3.4	1.2
Egypt, Arab Rep. of	32,501	160	2.5	1.2
El Salvador	3,390	290	3.7	1.9
Ethiopia	24,769	under 100	2.0	2.3
Ghana	8,341	190	2.5	0.0
Guinea	3,890	under 100	2.7	2.6
Haiti	4,768	under 100	2.0	−1.0
Honduras	2,495	260	3.4	1.1
India	526,043	110	2.3	1.1
Indonesia	116,600	100	2.4	0.8
Ivory Coast	4,942	240	2.8	4.7
Jordan	2,242	280	3.2	4.7
Kenya	10,890	130	3.1	1.5
Khmer Republic	7,284	130	3.3	0.5
Korea (North)	13,300	280	2.6	5.9
Korea, Republic of	31,139	210	2.6	6.4
Laos	2,893	110	2.4	0.2
Liberia	1,480	200	2.8	1.3
Malagasy Republic	6,656	110	2.4	0.0
Malawi	4,398	under 100	2.6	1.0
Mali	4,881	under 100	2.1	1.2
Mauritania	1,136	140	2.2	4.6
Morocco	15,050	190	2.9	3.4
Mozambique	7,539	210	1.8	3.3
Nepal	10,845	under 100	1.8	0.4
Niger	3,909	under 100	3.0	−0.9
Nigeria	64,560	under 100	2.6	−0.3
Pakistan (pre-war)	126,740	110	2.7	2.9

VERY POOR COUNTRIES (*Continued*)

	Popu-lation (add 000)	GNP Per Capita (US $)	GROWTH RATES	
			Pop'n (%)	GNP Per Capita (%)
Papua and New Guinea	2,363	210	2.4	2.0
Paraguay	2,314	240	3.1	1.0
Philippines	35,900	210	3.1	1.9
Rhodesia	5,090	240	3.2	0.4
Rwanda	3,650	under 100	3.1	−0.8
Senegal	3,790	200	2.2	−0.1
Sierra Leone	2,510	170	2.0	1.2
Somalia	2,730	under 100	2.5	1.5
Sudan	15,186	110	2.9	0.6
Syria, Arab Rep. of	5,866	260	2.8	4.7
Tanzania	12,557	under 100	2.6	1.6
Thailand	35,128	160	3.1	4.7
Togo	1,896	100	2.6	0.0
Tunisia	4,919	230	3.0	2.1
Uganda	9,500	110	3.0	1.7
Upper Volta	5,278	under 100	2.2	0.1
Viet-nam (North)	21,340	under 100	3.2	3.2
Viet-nam (South)	17,867	140	2.7	1.8
Yemen	5,556	under 100	2.1	2.3
Yemen, People's Rep.	1,220	120	2.2	−4.6
Zambia	4,020	290	2.6	5.4

For comparison, note some rich countries in the same year:

Germany, Federal Rep. of	60,842	2,190	1.0	3.7
Japan	102,322	1,430	1.0	10.0
United States	203,213	4,240	1.3	3.2
USSR	240,333	1,200	1.3	5.6

Author's Notes

The quotation of Mrs. Janice Bradshow, facing Chapter 1, is from *Poverty in America*, Margaret Gordon, ed. (San Francisco: Chandler Publishing Co., 1965), p. 426.

Chapter 1: On Seeing and Not Seeing the Poor

1. For example, Jeffrey Hadden, *The Gathering Storm in the Churches* (Garden City: Anchor Books, 1970), Chapter III.

2. Baltimore: Penguin Books, 1963.

3. Yet even these received some help from such measures as the Homestead Acts, which, significantly, excluded freed blacks.

4. It should be noted that the poor of the Depression did not "pull themselves up by their own bootstraps." Massive federal legislation helped considerably, and the mobilization of World War II finally ended the Depression.

5. 25 million Americans are classed as poor, even with a conservative accounting. See the Appendix for a note on the "poverty level" and how the estimates are made. Percentagewise, there probably is less poverty today in America than ever before, but the poverty-picture has altered significantly. For an analysis of this new poverty, see Oscar Ornati, *Poverty Amid Affluence* (New York: The Twentieth Century Fund, 1966).

6. Between 1950 and 1965 technology increased farm output by 45%

and farm labor decreased 45%. The President's National Advisory Commission on Rural Poverty has concluded that urban riots have their roots in rural poverty. Arthur Blaustein and Roger Woock, eds., *Man Against Poverty* (New York: Random House, 1968), p. 184.

7. In 1950 white-collar jobs were 37.5% of the total; in 1971 they were 48.6% and rising. *Statistical Abstract of the United States* (Washington: Department of Commerce). 1971 volume, Table 348; 1964, Table 307.

In 1971 the unemployment rate for all workers was 5.9%. The blue-collar rate was 7.4%. (Allentown) *Evening Chronicle*, April 7, 1972.

8. It should be noted that hundreds of thousands of workers make less with their jobs than they would receive on welfare. In New York City, for example, a 1969 estimate put 30% of the labor force with less than $90 a week before deductions. *New York Times*, Dec. 21, 1969.

One of the common myths concerning welfare in America is that welfare rolls are filled with able-bodied loafers. Of those on welfare, 55.5% are children, 18.6% are mothers, 15.6% are aged, and 9.4% are blind or disabled. Less than 1% are able-bodied unemployed males. Nixon administration statistics, *New York Times*, Nov. 28, 1971.

Frank Riessman, in his *Strategies Against Poverty* (New York: Random House, 1969), argues for "new careers" as the best way to combat poverty. He argues that even when jobs are available for the poor, they are seldom personally fulfilling. Often in urban riots, for example, employed men are the nucleus (in the Detroit riot, 80% of the rioters were employed). Not make-work "jobs" but "careers" are needed; we must work to develop many new meaningful careers, help the poor to qualify, and make sure that salaries are appropriate.

9. *New York Times*, April 2, 1972. Another aspect of social security is that in its collection procedures it is a "soak the poor" tax, rather than progressive like the income tax. With the present wage base of $9000, everyone below this pays 5.2%. But the percentage of total earnings taxed decreases as wages rise above $9000. Thus social security is doubly discriminatory for the poor, it taxes working poor more heavily, and it pays older poor less.

The hearings of the Special Committee on Aging of the Senate (U.S. Government Printing Office, 1970) are revealing. In 1968, median incomes for husbands and wives with no children at home were $8,752 for those under 65 and $4,038 for those 65 and over. Older women living alone or with nonrelatives have an especially hard time, with a 1968 median income of $1,670.

10. A classic study is John Dollard, *Caste and Class in a Southern Town* (New Haven: Yale University Press, 1937).

11. Gordon Allport, *The Nature of Prejudice* (Garden City: Anchor Books, 1954), is a comprehensive survey.

12. Commenting on the 1930's, Gunnar Myrdal noted, "On the contrary, in many instances there has been pronounced discrimination against the Negro. Negroes have often found it more difficult to receive any relief at all than whites in similar economic circumstances. Moreover, average relief grants per client have often been smaller for Negroes than they have been for whites. . . ." *The American Dilemma* (New York: Harper and Row, 1944 and 1962), p. 354.

13. *Time*, Feb. 8, 1971; *U.S. News and World Report*, June 14, 1971.

14. In footnote 8 we noted the "new careers" strategy. Now we come to the "welfare crisis" strategy. Frances Fox Piven and Richard A. Cloward have argued that America has never responded to the needs of the poor but has responded when the poor make trouble (e.g., the 30's and early 60's). Thus the poor must keep the pressure on by filling the welfare rolls and forcing change. They note that hundreds of thousands of Americans are eligible now but are not on the rolls, and they must be signed up. See Piven and Cloward, *Regulating the Poor: The Functions of Public Welfare* (New York: Pantheon Books, 1971). This is the rationale back of the National Welfare Rights Organization, which we will discuss in · Chapter 4.

15. The bill being negotiated by President Nixon, Representative Wilbur Mills, and Senator Abraham Ribicoff would do away with AFDC and substitute a Family Assistance Plan with a guaranteed income. Nixon first proposed a $1,600 floor; Mills would set it at $2,400, and Ribicoff at $3,000. Included would be a number of changes as part of the package. The increase in costs over present welfare expenditures would be between $10 and $25 billion. Key points of contention are the amounts to be guaranteed and the question of whether to require work on the part of recipients, especially mothers. We shall look at the work ethic in Chapter 2.

16. "Culture-Protestantism" is a term often used to describe a Protestant tendency, but it is appropriate to expand it to "Christian" here. Catholics in the twentieth century have "arrived" as far as American life is concerned and have often been so concerned with being American that they have unfortunately become very much like their Protestant neighbors.

17. An excellent survey is given by William G. McLoughlin, "Changing Patterns of Protestant Philanthropy, 1607–1969," in Donald R. Cutler, ed., *The Religious Situation: 1969* (Boston: Beacon Press, 1969).

18. *The Yearbook of American Churches* (New York: National Council of Churches, 1972) lists total giving to religious institutions in 1970 as $8.2 billion.

19. *New York Times*, April 23, 1970; the study concerned health and welfare ministries of the church.

20. W. Miller, in Louis German, Joyce Kornbluh, and Alan Haber, eds., *Poverty in America* (Ann Arbor: University of Michigan Press, 1965), p. 262.

21. Rokeach, "Value Systems in Religion," *Review of Religious Research*, Vol. 11, no. 1 (Fall 1969). Rokeach goes on, "The findings suggest that those who place a high value on *salvation* are conservative, are anxious to maintain the *status quo*, and are generally more indifferent and unsympathetic with the plight of the black and the poor."

Chapter 2: Paths Along the American Way

1. New York: Random House, 1970. Pp. 14, 16.

2. See Gustaf Wingren, *Luther on Vocation* (Philadelphia: Muhlenberg Press, 1957).

3. Hannah Arendt, *The Human Condition* (Garden City: Doubleday and Company, 1959), Chapter III.

4. This is one of the themes in John Kenneth Galbraith's *The New Industrial State* (New York: Signet Books, 1967). "The small volume of saving by the average man, and its absence among the lower-income masses, reflect faithfully the role of the individual in the industrial system and the accepted view of his function. The individual serves the industrial system not by supplying it with savings and the resulting capital; he serves it by consuming its products. On no other matter, religious, political or moral, is he so elaborately and skillfully and expensively instructed" (p. 49).

5. An exception is David M. Potter, *People of Plenty* (Chicago: University of Chicago Press, 1954). 1970 expenditures on advertising were nearly $20 billion; from 1971 *Statistical Abstract*, Table 1215.

6. See "The Importance of Being Carnal," Sam Keen, *To a Dancing God* (New York: Harper and Row, 1970).

7. Examples are Jacques Ellul, *The Technological Society* (New York: Vintage Books, 1964); Victor C. Ferkiss, *Technological Man: The Myth and the Reality* (New York: George Braziller, 1969); and Alvin Toffler, *Future Shock* (New York: Bantam Books, 1970).

8. Toffler and Ferkiss bypass poverty in their books. Reich hails technology as a tool for overcoming poverty if our consciousness can be transformed to "III." Proponents of the "Green Revolution" hail technological breakthroughs as a solution to world poverty (see Chapter 5).

9. Reich gives a rosy analysis in *The Greening of America*. A more critical approach is Theodore Roszak, *The Making of a Counter Culture* (Garden City: Anchor Books, 1969).

10. Neuhaus, *In Defense of People* (New York: Macmillan, 1971).

Chapter 3: The Marks of a Christian Consciousness

1. Cox, "The 'New Breed' in American Churches," in W. G. McLoughlin and R. N. Bellah, eds., *Religion in America* (Boston: Houghton Mifflin, 1968), p. 375.

2. Amos 5:11–12. All references from the Revised Standard Version.

3. *Old Testament Theology* (New York: Harper and Row, 1962), Vol. I, p. 400.

4. Jude 12; I Corinthians 16:1.

5. Acts 4:32–35.

6. For a solid study see Hans Conzelmann, *The Theology of St. Luke* (London: Faber and Faber, 1960).

7. Luke 1:51–52; also 4:18; 6:20; 12:16; 19:19.

8. John Pairman Brown, *The Liberated Zone* (Richmond: John Knox Press, 1969), p. 74. A similar approach is taken by Colin Morris, *Unyoung-Uncolored-Unpoor* (Nashville: Abingdon Press, 1969). Brown identifies Jesus with "revolutionary nonviolence" but Morris, who is president of the United Church of Zambia, is sympathetic with African revolutionaries in Rhodesia and sees Jesus condoning violence. Back of both books is the larger work by S. G. F. Brandon, *Jesus and the Zealots* (Manchester: Manchester University Press, 1967), who sets as his theme, "Think not that I came to bring peace on the earth. I came not to bring peace, but a sword" (Matthew 10:34). Brandon concludes that Jesus was not a fighter but that he was in basic sympathy with the rebel Zealots.

9. Eschatology literally means "a discourse about the last things." In New Testament terms it refers to the Kingdom of God and the coming reign of God. In our century a distinction is often made between "futurist eschatology" (the coming Kingdom and the primary concern of Jesus) and "realized eschatology" (emphasis on the presence of the Kingdom here and now). We shall return to this in Chapter 6.

10. Gibson Winter, *Elements for a Social Ethic* (New York: Macmillan, 1966), p. 255.

11. "Value is the *good-for-ness* of being for being in their reciprocity, their animosity, and their mutual aid. Value cannot be defined or intuited in itself for it has no existence in itself; and nothing is valuable in itself, but everything has value, positive or negative, in its relations." Niebuhr, *Radical Monotheism and Western Culture* (New York: Harper and Brothers, 1960), p. 107.

12. *The Responsible Self* (New York: Harper and Row, 1963), p. 56.

13. *I and Thou* (New York: Charles Scribner's Sons, 1958), p. 11.

14. *Church Dogmatics* (Edinburgh: T. and T. Clark, 1960), III/2, section 45.

15. The first assembly at Amsterdam in 1948 said: "A responsible society is one where freedom is the freedom of men who acknowledge responsibility to justice and social order, and where those who hold political authority or economic power are responsible for its exercise to God and the people whose welfare is affected by it"—*The First Assembly of the World Council of Churches: The Official Report* (New York: Harper and Brothers, 1949), pp. 77–80.

16. The term is from Jacques Ellul, *Violence* (New York: The Seabury Press, 1969), p. 67.

17. An example of the use of analogy is Roger Mehl, "The Basis of Christian Social Ethics," in John C. Bennett, ed., *Christian Social Ethics in a Changing World* (New York: Association Press, 1966).

Chapter 4: The Voices of the Poor

1. Richard Rogin, "Now It's Welfare Lib," *New York Times Magazine*, Sept. 27, 1970. Also, pamphlets from the NWRO.

2. Printed in Robert S. Lecky and Elliott H. Wright, eds., *Black Manifesto* (New York: Sheed and Ward, 1969).

3. For example, private property is seldom spoken of today as a natural right, but instead it is defended as a wise bit of social practice. At one time it was one of the major natural rights.

4. The Piven-Cloward strategy to end poverty, which we noted in Chapter I, emphasizes this legal right and encourages the poor to get every bit which the law allows.

5. Frantz Fanon sounds a similar note, "We say to ourselves: 'It's a just reparation which will be paid to us.' Nor will we acquiesce in the help for underdeveloped countries being a program of 'sisters of charity.' This help should be the ratification of a double realization: the realization by the colonized peoples that *it is their due* and the realization by the capitalist powers that in fact *they must pay*." *The Wretched of the Earth* (New York: Grove Press, 1963), p. 103.

6. Researcher Martin A. Larson's estimate, synagogues included. Another study has shown that seven major Protestant denominations hold $3 billion in stocks and bonds. Further, gifts to religious institutions in 1970 amounted to $8.2 billion. Charles W. Powers, *Social Responsibility and Investments* (Nashville: Abingdon, 1971), p. 129. Also *American Report*, Oct. 9, 1970 and *New York Times*, April 13, 1971.

7. This is a major insight of the manifesto: "The white Christian churches are another form of government in this country. . . ." Perhaps it pays too big a compliment to the churches because it places them be-

side government and business as part of the triumvirate of national power.

From our foregoing discussion of the manifesto, an outright endorsement is not implied. To reject the manifesto is inexcusable; but to enter into dialogue with it, perhaps offering alternative proposals for collection and use of funds, is quite responsible. William Stringfellow notes, "This does not mean that the original scheme, set forth in April 1969 at the Detroit Conference and subsequently brought into some white congregations and presented to some white ecclesiastical councils and assemblies, is or should be immune from criticism. It does mean, to my mind, that the relevant criticism of the Black Manifesto must be directed to its modesty, to its indefiniteness, and to the tentativeness with which it has been advanced, rather than to its substance or to its fundamental rationalization, either legally or theologically." (Lecky and Wright, p. 53.)

The manifesto has had a stimulating effect. So far the NBEDC has collected only $300,000, but it has shaken loose millions from the churches. The United Presbyterians have begun a campaign for $70 million for a Fund for the Self-Development of People. United Methodists recently voted $4 million and the Christian Church (Disciples) has doubled a $2 million program. The U.S. Catholic bishops have set up a $50 million campaign. *Time*, May 3, 1971; *New York Times*, June 7, 1970.

8. Ernst B. Haas, *The Web of Interdependence: The U.S. and International Organizations* (Englewood Cliffs: Prentice-Hall, 1970), p. 85.

The UN has subsequently launched a drive to translate the declaration into covenants binding on those nations which will ratify them. The U.S., while consistently supporting the moral rhetoric of rights, unfortunately has been cool to any covenant because this would involve some small sacrifice of sovereignty and might bring investigators into the country. The U.S. Senate hardly seems likely to pass any such covenant.

9. Printed in D. D. Raphael, ed., *Political Theory and the Rights of Man* (London: Macmillan, 1967).

10. *Seven Great Encyclicals* (Glen Rock, N.J.: Paulist Press, 1963). Other authors who speak of natural moral rights are Philip Wogaman, who speaks of a guaranteed income as a universal moral right, and Erich Fromm who says, "This right to live, to have food, shelter, medical care, education, etc., is an intrinsic human right that cannot be restricted by any condition, not even the one that he must be socially 'useful.' " Wogaman, *Guaranteed Annual Income: The Moral Issues* (Nashville: Abingdon Press, 1968), p. 88. Fromm, "The Psychological Aspects of the Guaranteed Income," in Theobald, Robert, ed., *The Guaranteed Income* (Garden City: Anchor Books, 1967), p. 184.

11. John 10:10.

12. Galatians 3:28.

13. These three interpretations of equality draw upon William K. Frankena, *Ethics* (Englewood Cliffs: Prentice-Hall, 1963), p. 39.

14. The 1970–71 school year was the first for open admissions, and it produced major changes in the 190,000-student university system, especially in its greatly enlarged freshman class. Compared with the year before, the black and Puerto Rican freshman enrollment increased by 123 percent, from 3,820 to 8,500; freshman enrollment for non-Puerto Rican whites grew by 64 percent, from 14,800 to 24,300. Open admissions is not new, for it has been found in some state university systems, notably California, but this is a great experiment because CUNY is surrounded by the poor. *New York Times*, March 26, 1971.

15. *Statistical Abstract.* Tables 500 and 503 of the 1971 volume and 443 of the 1962 volume.

16. America's concern "has primarily focused its attention on the poverty of insufficiency rather than the poverty of inequality." It has been presupposed that the poor would be helped if the entire pie were expanded, giving them a slice larger, although proportionally the same. Ornati, p. 2.

17. Myrdal, *The Challenge of World Poverty* (New York: Pantheon Books, 1970), pp. 52–54. Myrdal takes strong exception to a Pakistani report which says, "A conflict exists . . . between the aim of growth and equality . . . the inequalities in income contribute to the growth of the economy, which makes possible a real improvement for the lower-income groups."

18. Nathan Glazer in Margaret S. Gordon, ed., *Poverty in America* (San Francisco: Chandler Publishing Co., 1965), p. 16.

19. *Fortune* in May 1968 (Vol. LXXXVII, No. 5) listed 153 Americans worth over $100 million. Clearly most represent families rich before 1900. In 1971, 21 major league baseball players received $90,000 or more in salaries (*New York Times*, March 28, 1971). In 1971 the head of the International Telephone and Telegraph Corporation received $812,494 in salary and the three top executives of the Ford Motor Company received over $500,000 in salaries and bonuses [(Allentown) *Morning Call*, April 8, 1972].

Chapter 5: Who Speaks for Everyman?

1. See the Appendix. Also Roger Revelle, "Technology and the World Population-Hunger Problem," National Council of Churches, mimeographed 1967. Education and Calorie statistics from mid-sixties. Refugee statistics from *New York Times*, April 21, 1971.

2. William Wipfler, "Latin America: U.S. Colony," *Christianity and Crisis*, April 3, 1972.

3. Quoted in Louis M. Colonnese, "The Latin American Church Today: North American Perceptions," *Worldview*, April 1970.

4. Revelle, *op. cit.*

5. James Avery Joyce, "The Population Bomb: Can the United Nations Defuse It?" *War/Peace Report*, April 1971.

6. Frankel, *India's Green Revolution* (Princeton: Princeton University Press, 1971), p. 197.

7. Myrdal, pp. 123–25.

8. Elliott, "Poverty 2000," *Study Encounter*, Vol. VII, No. 3 (1971). Such a view is championed by Robert McNamara, head of the World Bank.

9. "Economic and Social Consequences of the Armaments Race," United Nations Document A/8469, October 1971. Figures are at 1970 prices. The UN study notes: "Military expenditures are in fact now running at two and a half times what all governments are spending on health, one and a half times what they spend on education, and 30 times more than the total of all official economic aid granted by developed to developing countries" (p. 16).

10. Wipfler, *op. cit.*

11. Myrdal, pp. 349, 456.

12. An additional $571,216,000 was budgeted for the Peace Corps, Inter-American Development Bank, World Bank, and other international agencies. From *Facts on File*, March 1972.

It is interesting to note that the U.S. spends about $3 billion a year on intelligence activities around the world through its CIA. *New York Times*, March 12, 1972.

13. Fulbright, *The Arrogance of Power* (New York: Vintage Books, 1966), Chapter 11. Myrdal, Chapter 11. *World Conference on Church and Society: Official Report* (Geneva: World Council of Churches, 1967), p. 209.

14. Fanon, p. 41. Mani was a third-century theologian who advocated a strongly dualistic view of the forces of evil *vs.* those of good. His view was rejected by most Christians.

15. John Gerassi, ed., *Revolutionary Priest: The Complete Writings and Messages of Camilo Torres* (New York: Vintage Books, 1971). Helder Camara, *The Church and Colonialism: The Betrayal of the Third World* (Denville, N.J.: Dimension Books, 1969). Stephen Bliss, "Christians for the Third World," *Christianity and Crisis*, April 3, 1972.

Violence is a hidden agenda in all discussions of poverty, and it is faced squarely by these men. Torres was a fighter, while Camara argues for passive resistance and is an admirer of Martin Luther King, Jr. All would agree, however, that a life of poverty is filled with inescapable violence, leaving the response even more difficult for those who abhor violence in all its forms.

16. The report concluded: "These facts and reflections move us to ask, respectfully and confidently, that our clergymen united in this assembly: (1) should not, in considering the problem of violence in Latin America, under any circumstances whatsoever compare or confuse the *unjust violence* of the oppressors, who maintain this odious system, with the *just violence* of the oppressed, who find themselves forced to use it to gain their liberation; (2) denounce with absolute clarity and no ambiguity the state of violence imposed by the powerful—be they individuals, groups, or nations—on the people of our region for centuries and proclaim the right of legitimate defense of the people; (3) exhort all Christians of Latin America, clearly and firmly, to work for everything that contributes to the real liberation of man in this area and to the establishment of a just and fraternal society in which all men will work together in good will; (4) assure all Christians a large measure of freedom in choosing the means best able to achieve this liberation and to create this society." (The report is printed in Gerassi, ed., pp. 442 ff.)

17. Wipfler, *op. cit.* William Wipfler is a former Latin American missionary of the Protestant Episcopal Church and now serves as Director of the Latin American Department of the National Council of Churches. He notes that "it is no coincidence that missionary expansion by U.S. churches has occurred precisely during those times when U.S. political and economic expansion has been most dynamic." Further, in the Roman Catholic Church much assistance was given to the Latin American Catholics and often the Catholic churches served as instruments of American intelligence and counterinsurgency efforts. This has been radically altered since the Medellin Conference in 1968. Today there are still 10,000 U.S. missionaries in Latin America, most of them from conservative Protestant mission groups; they exhibit an evangelical zeal seasoned with anticommunist ideology and are usually befriended by rightist military rulers.

18. Harry M. Caudill, *Night Comes to the Cumberlands* (Boston: Little, Brown, 1962). Clark, *Dark Ghetto* (New York: Harper and Row, 1965).

Chapter 6: On Starting the Extra Mile

1. *Agape* is used because it is the distinctive Greek New Testament word for Christian love. The discussion here reflects the insights of Anders Nygren, Karl Barth, and Reinhold Niebuhr.

2. Paul Ramsey comments on this approach: "God or Jesus Christ is introduced as an unexplained cipher, an opening paragraph, a pious platitude, a citation from scripture, or a little bit of ideology to set the tone. All the while the substantive analysis proceeds as it probably would were no such terms ever used. Nothing or very little is drawn out of Christian premises."—"Protestant Casuistry Today," *Christianity and Crisis*, Vol. XXIII, No. 3 (March 4, 1963).

3. Matthew 25:40.

4. Helmut Gollwitzer, *The Rich Christian and Poor Lazarus* (New York: Macmillan, 1970), p. 5.

5. *Ibid.*, p. 14.

6. "Pastoral Constitution on the Church in the Modern World," Section 39; from Walter M. Abbott, S.J., ed., *The Documents of Vatican II* (New York: Guild Press, 1966).

7. *The Future of Roman Catholic Theology* (Philadelphia: Fortress Press, 1970), p. 49.

8. This is the point at which Reich's "Consciousness III" falls short. We may agree with his analysis and criticism of American life, but his unabashed optimism and confidence in the consciousness of students is unjustified. His is a simple humanism of the eighteenth-century liberal kind, which knows little of the limits of man's nature and the need for grace.

9. Gustafson, *The Church as Moral Decision-Maker* (Philadelphia: Pilgrim Press, 1970), p. 152. Morality and ethics are overlapping terms, and I have chosen the latter. Morality focuses upon customs (mores) or accepted principles and patterns of behavior and how they relate to action. Ethics focuses more upon human nature, character, and consciousness; ethical reasoning seeks from a slightly different perspective to discern the rightness of a particular action. In everyday usage, the two terms are often interchangeable.

10. *God the Future of Man* (New York: Sheed and Ward, 1968), p. 126.

11. Empie, *Inside L.W.A.* (New York: Lutheran World Action, 1970), p. 5.

12. I myself am not a member of a traditional congregation but am part of what would be classed an underground group. Many such groups are not antichurch but are small avant-garde churches, concerned with church renewal and experimentation.

13. Cynthia Wedel, President of the National Council of Churches, notes: "But have we been right in our cavalier disdain for and disregard of the vast number of earnest church members whom we have left bewildered and angry? Are we, not they, primarily responsible for the polarization which is undermining effective social action on the part of the

churches?"—"The Church and Social Action," *The Christian Century*, Aug. 12, 1970.

14. Gustafson, pp. 155–56.

15. M. Darrol Bryant, *To Whom It May Concern* (Philadelphia: Fortress Press, 1969), p. 33.

16. Drucker, p. 226.

17. Lyle E. Schaller, "The Churches and the Challenges of Poverty," in Kendig B. Cully and F. Nile Harper, eds., *Will the Church Lose the City?* (New York: World Publishing Co., 1969).

18. Lillian B. Rubin, "Maximum Feasible Participation," *The Annals of the American Academy of Political and Social Science*, Vol. 385 (September 1969). The program is still operating in many urban centers.

19. A discussion of some of these church programs is found in Lyle E. Schaller, *The Churches' War on Poverty* (Nashville: Abingdon, 1967). A solid work along these lines is also Meryl Ruoss, *Citizen Power and Social Change: The Challenge to Churches* (New York: Seabury Press, 1968).

20. Gollwitzer, p. 94.

Appendix: Some Statistics

1. *New York Times*, January 10 and May 8, 1971.

2. *Social Security Bulletin*, June 1971, Table M-22.

3. *Ibid.*, Tables M-24, M-25.

4. "World Bank Atlas," (Washington: International Bank for Reconstruction and Development, 1971).

Selected Bibliography

Bennett, John C., ed. *Christian Social Ethics in a Changing World.* New York: Association Press, 1966. Twenty articles by social ethicists, prepared for the Geneva conference.

Brown, John Pairman. *The Liberated Zone: A Guide to Christian Resistance.* Richmond: John Knox Press, 1969. A number of topics covered by a radical American Protestant.

Bryant, M. Darrol. *A World Broken by Unshared Bread.* Geneva: World Council of Churches, 1970. Commissioned by the youth of the Lutheran World Federation.

Camara, Dom Helder. *Revolution Through Peace.* New York: Harper and Row, 1971. A Brazilian Archbishop who is an outspoken champion of the poor.

Castel, Helene, ed. *World Development: An Introductory Reader.* New York: Macmillan, 1971. Variety of essays sponsored by the Methodists.

Clark, Henry. *The Christian Cast Against Poverty.* New York: Association Press, 1965. A readable little volume; includes historical background as well as a response to conservatives.

Clark, Kenneth B. *Dark Ghetto*. New York: Harper and Row, 1965. A must for understanding urban poverty; by a highly respected black social psychologist.

Fanon, Frantz. *The Wretched of the Earth*. New York: Grove Press, 1963. A highly influential book by the late eloquent black spokesman for revolutionary consciousness.

Gerassi, John, ed. *Revolutionary Priest: The Complete Writings and Messages of Camilo Torres*. New York: Vintage Books, 1971. Torres was a Colombian priest who died in 1966 as a guerrilla fighter. Other key Latin American documents.

Gollwitzer, Helmut. *The Rich Christian and Poor Lazarus*. New York: Macmillan, 1970. By a prominent German theologian.

Hadden, Jeffrey K. *The Gathering Story in the Churches*. Garden City: Anchor Books, 1970. A sociologist looks at the growing gap between activist leaders and the more conservative average churchgoer.

Kotz, Nick. *Let Them Eat Promises: The Politics of Hunger in America*. Englewood Cliffs: Prentice-Hall, 1969. Analysis of the Johnson and Nixon policies.

Lecky, Robert S., and Wright, H. Elliott, eds. *Black Manifesto*. New York: Sheed and Ward, 1969. Defense of the manifesto, with key documents.

McLoughlin, William G. "Changing Patterns of Protestant Philanthropy, 1607–1969," *The Religious Situation, 1969*, ed. Donald R. Cutler. Boston: Beacon Press, 1969. An enlightening article, well-documented.

Morris, Colin. *Unyoung, Uncolored, Unpoor*. Nashville: Abingdon, 1969. A no-holds-barred indictment of the churches by one whose home is Africa.

Moynihan, Daniel P., ed. *On Understanding Poverty*. New York: Basic Books, 1968. Twelve scholarly articles from the social science establishment.

Myrdal, Gunnar. *The Challenge of World Poverty: A World Anti-Poverty Program in Outline*. New York: Pantheon Books,

1970. Policy evaluations of his massive *Asian Drama* by one of the great masters of socio-economic study.

Ornati, Oscar. *Poverty Amid Affluence.* New York: The Twentieth Century Fund, 1966. Overview of many aspects of poverty, good on definitions and defining of the problems.

Paul VI (Pope). *Populorum Progressio (On the Development of Peoples).* Washington: National Catholic Welfare Conference, 1967. A great post-Vatican II encyclical.

Piven, Frances Fox, and Cloward, Richard A. *Regulating the Poor.* New York: Pantheon Books, 1971. History of American welfare efforts since the thirties with some proposals by the champions of the crisis strategy.

Potter, David M. *People of Plenty: Economic Abundance and the American Character.* Chicago: University of Chicago Press, 1954. Helpful in interpreting middle-class America.

Powers, Charles W. *Social Responsibility and Investments.* Nashville: Abingdon, 1971. How the churches may influence American corporations through their investment policies.

Riessman, Frank. *Strategies Against Poverty.* New York: Random House, 1969. Critique of the approaches of Alinsky, Cloward/Piven, and Moynihan, and a development of Riessman's "new careers" approach.

Rokeach, Milton. "Value Systems in Religion," *Review of Religious Research.* vol. XI, no. 1 (Fall 1969). A psychologist looks at churchgoers; bad news.

Ruoss, Meryl. *Citizen Power and Social Change: The Challenge to Churches.* New York: Seabury, 1968. How the churches may deal with power and social structures.

Schaller, Lyle E. *The Churches' War on Poverty.* Nashville: Abingdon, 1967. Case studies on how churches have become involved, especially in cooperation with some government programs.

Simon, Arthur. *Breaking Bread with the Hungry.* Minneapolis: Augsburg Publishing House, 1971. Chapters on the population crisis and the Green Revolution.

Theobald, Robert, ed. *The Guaranteed Income*. New York: Anchor Books, 1966. Ten articles—psychological, sociological, and economic approaches.

Thurman, Howard. *Jesus and the Disinherited*. Nashville: Abingdon, 1949. An older passionate appeal from a Protestant liberal.

Wogaman, Philip. *Guaranteed Annual Income: The Moral Issues*. Nashville: Abingdon, 1968. Good treatment by a Protestant ethicist.

World Conference on Church and Society: Official Report. Geneva: World Council of Churches, 1967. The groundbreaking 1966 Geneva conference where the poor had major spokesmen.

World Development: The Challenge to the Churches. Geneva: Exploratory Committee on Society, Development and Peace, 1968. Report of the 1968 Beirut conference where Catholic, Orthodox, and Protestant Christians wrestled with our problem.